IT'S A BIRD, IT'S A PLANE... IT'S A STAIN!

It has the power to interrupt any event, any thought, or any plan. It can destroy something of great value in seconds, and give you a quiet punch that marks you more than a black eye. . . .

Bestselling author Don Aslett, founder of his own multi-million-dollar janitorial service, tells you how to remove more than 200 of the toughest stains from every imaginable surface . . . from blusher to burn marks, spaghetti sauce, and shoe polish, from the coffee spilled on your car's new upholstery to the Kool-Aid stain (red, of course) on your formerly beige carpet to that menacing "mystery stain." This lively, practical guide will show you how to eliminate all those little (and not so little) stains, smudges, and splotches from your otherwise spotless world!

Don Aslett's STAINBUSTER'S BIBLE

DON ASLETT is the bestselling author of *Clutter's Last Stand, Is There Life After Housework?* and *How Do I Clean the Moosehead?* (available in a Plume edition).

ALSO BY DON ASLETT

Is There Life After Housework?

Do I Dust or Vacuum First?

Clutter's Last Stand

Who Says It's a Woman's Job to Clean?

Make Your House Do the Housework

Pet Clean-Up Made Easy

Cleaning Up for a Living

Is There a Speech Inside You?

How Do I Clean the Moosehead?

Don Aslett's

STAIN-BUSTER'S BIBLE

The Complete Guide to Spot Removal

DON ASLETT

Illustrated by Craig LaGory

A PLUME BOOK

PLUME
Published by the Penguin Group
Penguin Books USA Inc., 375 Hudson Street, New York,
New York 10014, U.S.A.
Penguin Books Ltd, 27 Wrights Lane, London W8 5TZ, England
Penguin Books Australia Ltd, Ringwood, Victoria, Australia
Penguin Books Canada Ltd, 2801 John Street, Markham,
Ontario, Canada L3R 1B4
Penguin Books (N.Z.) Ltd, 182-190 Wairau Road, Auckland 10,
New Zealand

Penguin Books Ltd, Registered Offices: Harmondsworth, Middlesex, England

First published by Plume, an imprint of Penguin Books USA Inc.
Published simultaneously in Canada.

First Printing, June, 1990
10 9 8 7 6 5 4 3 2 1

Ⓟ REGISTERED TRADEMARK—MARCA REGISTRADA

Library of Congress Cataloging in Publication Data
 Aslett, Don, 1935–
   [Stainbuster's bible]
   Don Aslett's stainbuster's bible : the complete guide to spot
 removal / by Don Aslett ; illustrated by Craig LaGory.
     p.   cm.
   ISBN 0-452-26384-0
   1. Spotting (Cleaning)   I. Title.   II. Title: Stainbuster's bible.
 TX324.A75835   1990
 648'.1—dc20   89-77091
                                                   CIP

Printed in the United States of America
Set in Century Expanded
Designed by Julian Hamer and Dan Rembert

Contents

**(The Mistakes That Turn Tiny Spots into
Big Stains)** The things you never want
to do to any stain, because they'll make
removal a lot harder . . . or hopeless. The six
greatest mistakes of would-be stain removers.

10 Prevent Those Stains!

(It's a Lot Easier Than Removing Them)
Helpers that could help—if we would only let
them. And some excellent habits to break.

Part II WHAT'S IT ON?

**(An Important Part of the Answer to "How
Do I Get It Out?")** The stainbuster's guide
to surface savvy—the right way to approach
all/each of the fabrics and surfaces most
frequently stained.

Part III HOW TO GO ABOUT IT

**(The Most Common Spots and Stains and
How to Remove Them)** An illustrated
handbook for undoing the most frequent
offenders.

A Note to Readers

If I've learned anything in more than thirty years of professional cleaning, it's that even with the best available method and materials in the most common ordinary cleaning situation, the result can boomerang on you. So we can't expect perfection in this volume or anywhere else.

If we bought a book on sex, on cooking, or on raising children, and it promised that after we read and applied it we'd never have a bad night or a bad batch of cookies, or that our kids would mind us perfectly for the rest of their lives, none of us would expect or believe it. There are too many things information alone can't predict or control. I've tried a never-fail campfire peach cobbler recipe in the mountains seven times now, for example, and each time that crumby, charcoaly mass has done worse than the time before. My wife and I had eight teenagers at home all at once not so long ago, and need I tell you that neither the best book nor a master's in child management could guarantee results.

So it is with spot and stain removal. I've had some stains come out in seconds, and under different conditions I couldn't get the very same stain off with sandpaper!

In these pages I've provided both the best of my own third of a century of stain- and spot-removal experience and that of a wide variety of other stain veterans, but I still can't promise every carpet, couch, or culotte will come completely clean every time. I can't guarantee every spot out every time, only that the odds for successful removal and of avoiding harm to the garment or surface will swing to your side. It's as if you called the doctor and said, "I don't feel good, Doc, what should I do?" "What's wrong?" "Well, I think it's my elbow again." What the doctor tells you to do depends a lot on **your** judgment and assessment of what's wrong. Likewise spots and stains are hard to diagnose via the printed page. I've tried to give you enough information to make the chances of recovery pretty promising. But just like the doctors, I do have to disclaim. I won't get the glory for your stainbusting triumphs, and unfortunately, I can't take responsibility for your failures, either.

Good Spotting,
Don Aslett

Introduction: There's a Stain Out There with Your Name on It!

"Help! My husband sweats heavily and the armpits of his leather coat are incredibly stained. How do I get it out?"

I've done several thousand radio and television interviews on cleaning, and no matter what I'm supposed to be discussing— floors, walls, bathroom cleaning, or clutter—I inevitably get questions like that. I can attempt to switch the conversation back to beating rugs, but once the stain bug is out, all the calls—at least ten in a row—are on spills, spots, stains, and the odors they create. I finally realized why—stains and spots are the emergency room of cleaning. All other cleaning can wait or be put on hold if it has to be. Overall cleaning is pretty low-key, but not stains and spots. They always happen at the wrong time and in the wrong place and we can't say I'll get you later. If they stay they set and ruin things, and we get tired of converting thirty-dollar shirts to workshirts.

We can fake, gloss, and polite our way over most unpleasant events—but not a stain. It talks right back to us: "Well, fumble fingers, everyone is wondering how you're going to handle this."

Here's some help!

In a lifetime we can expect an average of fifty thousand spots, stains, and spills.

Lord Willingham can just move to a new castle when custard spills on the carpet. Darryl Strawberry can throw his suits away when they get stained. If Madonna had a stained blouse a million teens would try to match it! And Donald Trump can simply buy a new building with a dry cleaner on the ground floor.

Unfortunately, most of us can't pull off any of those tricks. We're stuck with the stains. All of which will come at the worst possible time and end up in the worst possible place. We all know how many seemingly innocent stainmakers are out there just itching for a chance to jump us. We know the bread always falls jelly side down, we know how it is with stains.

- They happen as soon as something comes back from the cleaners, not before it goes in.

- We get them on the way to town, never on the way home.

- A stain will never hit a sleeve if a crotch or a bosom is available.

- It's always in the middle, never on the edge.

- The red tapers never drip until they're on Aunt Emily's lace tablecloth.

- The baby won't feel like burping until we get dressed up.

- Bloody beef or overripe watermelon will be served on a one-ply paper plate.

- The TV dinner that explodes on opening will be the one with indelible sauce.

- Nobody ever slops red wine on a burgundy rug.

- We can puree beets in the blender with the lid off wearing anything we don't care about.

- Cars miss mud puddles until we walk by them.

- Nosebleeds know when you're wearing Dry Clean Only.

- We won't brush up against the door latch unless we're wearing our white linen skirt.

- Cooking grease can always find the part of our anatomy the apron doesn't cover.

- It'll always fall on the leg that you lead with.

- They won't forget to hold the mayo unless it really matters.

- The boss will bring up your future with the company over a Hawaiian buffet.

- The pizza sauce won't land on the photocopy.

- The spot will be in the part that you iron last.

And on top of all that, we don't get the old easy stains of our forefathers, we get Space Age spots! We've developed more spot and stain sources since 1935 than they had in all 13,975 years previous (even counting chariot manure and axle grease).

Not too long ago, mud, grass, grease, hard candy, and cocoa were about it. Today we come up against thousands of chemicals, hundreds of drinks, inks, paints, sprays, foods, condiments, coatings, lubricants, and cosmetics. Spots and stains are as inevitable as flus and taxes—and no one is exempted. They hit the rich as well as the poor and observe true equality of sexes as they follow us faithfully from the cradle to the nursing home. If we don't cause it, someone else will spill it on us or our property. No life is secure enough, no possession so well hidden it can escape the long arms of stains. We have cells and corpuscles to help get germs and viruses out of our life, but there's nothing that kicks in after the splat of chocolate pie lands in our lap. When it comes to spots and stains, we're on our own as soon as they're on us!

Stainbuster's Bible to the Rescue!

Dropping your coffee cup is a lot like taking a spill on your ten-speed—it's the landing that hurts, not the fall. Quick, expert first aid is the answer to both. In the case of stains, if you know what to use and how to use it you can minimize if not eliminate the damage. With the information in this little volume, anyone can become an expert at removing common everyday stains. Just knowing what to do and doing it in time can make most spots easy to manage.

And once you learn to get them out:

- You won't have to wait for a week to wear it or get it back from the cleaners.

- You can cope with it when disaster strikes the only white shirt you have with you on the trip, or your party dress when you haven't even reached the party.

- There's a much better chance of actually getting it out if you can do it yourself right on the spot. Time sets most stains, and some spots you just can't get to the dry cleaner fast enough to avoid permanent damage.

- And even if it needs a pro, you'll know what to do to keep it from getting worse while help is on the way.

- You'll save money by not rushing everything down to the dry cleaners. They deserve your business, but for all your spots? Impossible! Not to mention all the money that won't be lost on ruined garments, finishes, and furnishings.

- Knowing how to handle stains at home or away can do a lot for human relations, too. (Including all those guest and grandkid stains.)

- You'll save time, mental anguish, and embarrassment.

- There's a lot of pride and satisfaction in being able to do your own stainbusting too!

So you can grin and wear it or grin and remove it. You really can.

Does it take a lot of knowledge and specialized chemicals to do this?

No, the instructions for removing each kind of stain are easy to follow and don't call for any special experience. The spotting equipment is all available at drug, hardware, or janitorial-supply stores. In these pages I'll teach you the secrets and techniques of the experts, the people who are up against serious stains every day—dry cleaners, professional launderers, carpet-cleaning technicians, chemists, manufacturers, and moms. I'll even tell you when to give up and call in the cavalry, or toss it to the quilt pile or the teenagers! But with a little care and practice, anyone can learn to take care of most spots and spills. Before you know it, you'll find yourself skillfully removing stains that once made you fear and tremble. And you'll be amazed how many blotches are Band-Aid simple to fix!

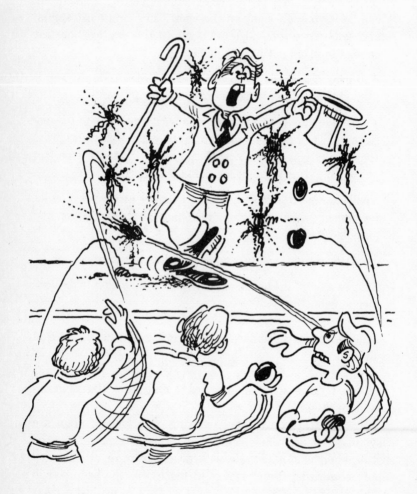

Are You Stain-Prone?

(Check your stain quotient: Do you have the hots for spots?)

A five-minute test to determine how many stains you invite daily. Put a check beside any of the following that you do.

☐ Own skirts/dresses/robes that reach the ground

☐ Own anything white, yellow, or light orange

☐ Have unfinished wood or unsealed concrete floors

☐ Don't use or believe in Scotchgard

☐ Have any unfixed leak

☐ Leave half-finished cups or cans of your favorite beverage around

☐ Feed pets in unauthorized places (at least sometimes)

☐ Think aprons are sissy

☐ Lay candy bars on the dash or seat of the car

☐ Choose raspberry or cherry every time

☐ Kneel in freshly cut lawn

☐ Try to carry bulging grocery bags one-handed

- ☐ Leave open anything on the stairs

- ☐ Believe there's anywhere you can set the nail polish bottle that's "spill proof"

- ☐ Lose track of the lid to anything

- ☐ Move a ladder with something on it

- ☐ Chew gum

- ☐ Smoke (you're guilty of at least thirty stains already)

- ☐ Lose pen caps the first day

- ☐ (For men only) Overshoot the bowl

- ☐ "Forget" to put down old newspapers before you clean the oven

- ☐ Like extra-long cuffs on sleeves or pants

- ☐ Have soup-dip-length hair, beard, or mustache

- ☐ Decide to dump it or pick it up later

- ☐ Wear white or suede shoes

- ☐ Can't be bothered to change into "painting clothes"

- ☐ Eat in traffic

- ☐ Eat while reading or working with papers

☐   Eat in the living room

☐   Eat over carpet anywhere

☐   Eat while asleep or half asleep

☐   Sneak-eat or "sample"

☐   Eat in bed or while lying down

☐   Eat in your lap

☐   Buffet-style eating

☐   Eat in cars, boats, or anything in motion

☐   Eat without a napkin, or with too small a napkin

☐   Eat without leaning forward

☐   Don't bother to blot your fingers after eating finger foods

☐   Gobble up any kind of greasy snack food

Count up the checks, give yourself one point per check, and tally up your score.

1–10 = We should all lead such a spotless life.

11–20 = I'm glad to see you only spend about half your time removing spots.

21–30 = Hope your dog is named Spot!

31–40 = You'll be reincarnated as a leopard.

How to Use This Book

There are other books out there on stains, but this one's different. Sure, the step-by-step procedures you need to remove life's most pesky stains are in here (in Part III, "How to Go About It"). And I've introduced you to all the stainbusting techniques you need to know to be really effective when a stain happens. There are also lists and descriptions of the tools and chemicals you need to be a real stain pro, and a professional rating of the "home remedies" for stains that often just make things worse. But a lot of these pages are devoted to helping you avoid all this work entirely!

Part I, for example, takes a hard look at stains and how they happen. It explains the simple rules for keeping ordinary spills from developing into problem stains. It gives you a guided tour of the whole landscape of stains and tells you how to make expert use of an ordinary old washing machine to dispose of three-quarters of them. It lets you know when the smartest move is to take it to the pros—or toss it in the trash. It tells you how to protect your clothing and other possessions from stain damage, and even how to avoid and prevent the most common and dangerous stains.

Part II is a directory of the different kinds of surfaces stains occur on, and how to handle each one. Because the stain is only half the story. The other, equally important half, is what's it **on**? There's a world of difference in handling a tomato sauce stain on a white cotton blouse, nylon carpeting, or an earth-tile floor. Before you start to remove a stain, don't just look up the procedure for that specific stain in "How to Go About It." Look up the particular surface it's on, too, in Part II. This will keep you aware of what to do and what not to do to that specific material, to avoid damage and disappointment. This section also gives you some insight into the relative stain-resistance of different fabrics and furnishings and building materials, to help you pick the ones that will keep you out of trouble.

I put Part III, "How to Go About It," at the end of the book, to help convince you to read the other parts first. I know how you would-be stainbusters think! You buy the book as a hedge against the day you drop the borscht on the dining room rug. But you don't read it yet, because who knows for sure what the big spill will be—it might be chocolate ice cream or Zinfandel. No sense in boning on borscht now, you may never get a chance to apply all that hard-earned knowledge. So you put the book on the shelf, and when the crisis occurs you grab it down quick and turn to "B" for borscht, right? Wrong! If you'll read at least Part I now, you may be able to avoid the catastrophe altogether, or at least make it less of a mess when it does happen. You want to equip yourself with the all important background information **now**—not when you're up to your ankles in beet soup. I can just see you sitting there asking yourself: "What do you suppose 'tamp' means and what does 'feather' have to do with all this?" So do yourself a favor. Read at least Part I, and maybe even Part II, and start assembling the tools and chemicals you'll need to be prepared. I don't expect you to sit down and read through all the "How to Go About It's" for everything from Acid to Wood Stain, but I hope you really will read the rest. Then, when the big spill happens, you'll be ready for it.

Speaking of Part III, I've tried to simplify it so that it isn't full of repetitive instructions. There are only so many ways to remove a stain, and a lot of different stains are handled the same way. So I've bunched the ones that are treated alike together. Lipstick and shoe polish are both removed the same way, for instance, so they both appear under one procedure. The surest way to find the removal instructions for a particular stain is to look that stain up in the index. All the stains in the book are listed here and cross-referenced, to make them easy to locate.

I've also geared the instructions in Part III toward the items we're most often trying to de-stain, and that generally turns out to be our clothing. We spill a lot of stuff on our carpets, too, for example, but we're not too keen on getting down there to clean them up. Unless a carpet spill is really noticeable, we often like to just walk on it awhile, until it blends in, and then try to hold out until the Steam Genie man comes. But let us get a smudge or spot on our white linen jacket or Brooks Brothers necktie, and it's instant stain warfare—can't have something around that makes such an obvious statement about our character, can we? I know, it's a little crazy, but that's why many of the stain-removal instructions are slanted toward spots on garments. It's easy to adjust the procedures for use on other surfaces, though, with the information I give you in Part II.

That takes care of my part, the rest is up to you. Happy stainbusting!

Part I

STAIN-BUSTER'S BASICS

1

DON'T DO THIS!

(The Mistakes That Turn Tiny Spots into Big Stains)

You had a tiny leak in your tire and you **ignored it**, so you had a blowout or a ruined tire. You tried to mop the floor without sweeping it, and ended up with mud and mashed Cheerio soup. You didn't **remove the worst of it first.** You put lawn-mower gas in a water jug, only to grab it when you needed a drink or to put out a fire. It's the **wrong stuff!** And who could forget the doctor who didn't **pretest** that patient and amputated the wrong arm. Then there was that small itchy spot you couldn't refrain from **rubbing** into a raging rash. What about the time you ended up with an aquarium full of boiled angelfish before you realized the **heat setting** was bad?

Your own life experience has already exposed you to the six deadly sins that make a stain worse. Let's take a closer look at them so we can keep those spots small!

The Six Deadly Sins— Guaranteed to Turn a Simple Spot into a Sinister Stain

• **Ignoring it.** Almost every stain is easier to remove when fresh. (The exceptions are things like mud and Play-Doh, which are best left to dry, so that most of the mess can be dry-brushed away.) But for most stains, the quicker you get started on them, the better your chance of success. A cola spill on the carpet is no sweat if you blot it up the minute it happens. If you let it go, the liquid soaks into the fibers and seeps down into the backing and pad and the sugars and caramel coloring set into a stain that won't be easy to remove, especially from the depths of the carpet. The same is true of pet stains. If treated right away with a bacteria/enzyme digester (see p. 63 and 260-263, all traces of the stain can be eliminated, but an old, dried pet stain in carpet is all but impossible.

Alcoholic beverages spilled on clothing can damage the fabric and be impossible to remove if left to dry (especially on wool)—which is why you always want to sponge alcohol spills off with water immediately. Ditto for coffee, cologne, perfume, and milk. Most oils (salad oil, mayonnaise, margarine, motor oil) will oxidize and set within a matter of days if not removed. When Fido eats a dead mouse and burps it up on the jogging suit you left on the bathroom floor, the impulse is to bundle it up and bury it in the bottom of the dirty clothes hamper. But you need to take a deep breath and rinse it out *now*—otherwise those strong stomach acids will bleach and permanently sully your sweats. **Quick action** is the single most important rule in spot removal—get 'em before they have a chance to become stains.

• **Not removing the worst of it first.** Why launch into chemical warfare on any part of a stain or spill you can just sweep, scrape, or vacuum away? The easily removable part is usually the **bulk** of it. Whether it's liquid or solid, you always want to get up as much as you can before using any spotters, even water. Remember: Spotters are solvents, made to **dissolve** the stain. If you have a blob of tar or grease on your coat, the last thing you want to do is apply solvent before removing as much of the tar or grease as you can. The dyes in a dab of tar, lipstick, or rouge can stain a mighty large area if you dilute it with solvent and start spreading it around. So remove as much of the deposit as possible while it's dry and intact, then use water or solvent to remove what little bit remains. It's amazing how much of a spot you can get out by just gently working it and being patient, before ever adding liquid of any kind.

With liquid spills, too—why try to chemically counteract 8 ounces of baby formula when you could blot or wet/dry vacuum 7.5 ounces of it up first? Liquid spills should be blotted up, and solids can be gently scraped up with a dull knife or spoon, or brushed off. Brittle residues can often be coaxed out by "flexing" the fabric—folding it over sharply in the area of the stain and rubbing it back and forth on itself. Fresh oily residues can be pulled out with an absorbent compound. Powders, such as copy machine toner, should be vacuumed. If you apply a liquid to unremoved powder you're going to witness a mighty migration of your spot! It's like putting water on dirt—you end up with mud. Take care not to smear any loose material around or drive it into the fabric in your attempts to remove it.

• **Using the wrong stuff.** I've done it dozens of times—gotten food, ink, or an airline terminal smudge on my suit or shirt traveling, and as soon as I get to the motel rub a bar of soap on it and start scrubbing it viciously. Then I give up, let it dry and take it home, and that stain is there for good!

It's critical to correctly identify what caused a stain and the material it's on before you start slathering chemicals on it. Ammonia can work wonders on blood and protein stains, but it can set coffee and make it permanent. Acetone will dissolve fingernail polish out of many fabrics, but will melt a hole in your acetate slip. Enzyme digesters can be very helpful for man-made fibers, but will attack silk and wool, as will chlorine bleach. Alcohol will bleed dyes from some fabrics. Even water will set many oily stains such as salad dressing and mustard. Take the time to be sure of what it was that caused the stain—don't just jump to conclusions—whether you plan to work on it yourself or take it to a pro. The care labels in clothes should let you know the type of fabric you're dealing with and how to handle it. (See p. 131-133.)

PRE-TEST

- **Forgetting to pretest.** With the hundreds of different kinds of fibers and blends around today, it's hard to always be sure what you're dealing with. So it's always a good idea to test (*that means practice, or experiment with!*) any spotting chemical in an inconspicuous area to make sure it won't damage the fabric or cause color change. Even plain water will pull dye out of some silks, and we'd rather have something like that happen in the seam allowance or hem of a garment than smack in the middle of it. Test carpeting on a remnant, or in a closet or other out-of-the-way place; upholstered furniture on the back or underside.

- **Rubbing and scrubbing it.** The first thing most of us want to do with a stain—it helps us feel like we're doing something. But it's dangerous for two reasons: It spreads the stain, and it can damage the surface we're trying to remove the stain from. We've all done it—started out with a tiny pen mark or grease spot, we're almost tempted to leave it alone, no one will notice. But it's like a scab or a missing chip of paint, we just can't let it be. Now it's noticeable, we know we goofed, so more speed, solution, and pressure. Before you know it we've rubbed the paint or finish right off!

We remove stains by gently "pulling" the stain agent out of the fabric, by blotting and flushing. If something more than that is needed, we use a gentle "tamping" or special scraping technique (see Chapter 5). Vigorous rubbing or scrubbing usually just makes a stain bigger and more obvious and harder to remove. Scrubbing will often bruise the fabric or fibers, too, leaving a pilled or fuzzy spot where you worked on it—or if the fabric is delicate, even an actual hole. These scrubbed spots will show and look bad, even if you get all the stain out, because the surface has been roughened and damaged. You want to avoid wringing stained fabrics, too, because this can distort the fabric as well as drive the stain deeper into the fibers.

- **Applying heat.** Many stains are "set" by heat. An otherwise removable stain will become impossible to get out when washed in hot water, dried in the clothes dryer, or ironed. When you're working on a stain, use a cold or warm water wash, and check to make sure the stain came out before throwing the item in the dryer. And if you wash your white socks with a red sweatshirt and get a "pink load," don't dry it (see p. 41). Always inspect "removed" stains carefully before ironing—the heat will often oxidize any remaining residue and turn it yellow.

Don't help innocent spots develop into permanent stains! Handling everyday spots and spills successfully doesn't take an expert, just somebody like you with a little common sense and a slower trigger finger.

DON'T EVER

- Ignore a stain or leave it till "later"

- Fail to take advantage of the fact that three quarters or more of the stain or spot can probably just be swept, scraped, or vacuumed away

- Apply water or **any** chemical until you're sure what the stain is and what it's on

- Forget to pretest

- Rub or scrub a stain

- Apply heat of any kind to a stain that isn't 100 percent removed

2

IT MIGHT JUST COME OUT IN THE WASH

(Wash It Out—
The Basic
Stain-Removal
Strategy
for Washables)

If most of the clothes you wear are washable, the majority of your stain skirmishes will be won or lost in the laundry room. Mating up with your Maytag might prove the smartest stain-prevention maneuver you ever made. Three out of four everyday stains can simply be washed out, if you just take a little extra time to identify and pre-treat spots before you toss everything in the top-loader. For washables, this is the easiest way to deal with all but problem stains. For fabrics and colors that tolerate hot water and chlorine bleach, even a lot of the tough stains will come out in the washer, including alcoholic beverages, coffee, milk, ice cream, cosmetics, grass stains, chocolate, egg, fruit juice, and gravy.

Here's how to build effective stain removal right into your regular laundry:

- **Stay aware of stains.** And make sure anyone else whose clothes you do makes you aware of them, so you can give them special attention. The heat of washing or drying will otherwise make many stains impossible ever to get out.

- **Don't wait till washday.** Most spots become more stubborn with age, and some are hard to see after they dry, so the safest approach is to tend to spots and spills as soon as they happen. Wash it right away if at all possible, because there's less chance of success with each passing day. It's worth a wash to save a twenty-eight-dollar pair of slacks from a brush with barbecue sauce (and there's always *something* in the hamper that could safely be used to fill out the load). That greasy red stain will only cost you a few minutes and about fifty cents to remove—what a bargain. If you can't wash right away, sponge fresh stains with plain water. At the very least, stick a safety pin on there so you remember that the sweater you're washing on Saturday still has half of Thursday's milkshake spilled down the front.

- When you come upon a stain, remember: **Always get rid of the worst of it first!** Knock it off, scrape it off, or brush it off. Gobs of grease, lumps of manure, and crusts of mud don't disappear in the wash, they're dissolved and circulated—so the less on a garment, or on anything being cleaned, the better the end result.

- **Pre-treat!** Most stains on washable items will benefit from pre-treatment (as described for each specific stain in Part III of this book—"How to Go About It"), followed by laundering in warm water. You can pre-treat while you're sorting the loads, as you're going through pockets, etc. This will give the pre-treat the few minutes it needs to sit on there before you load the machine (see p. 35-36 for more on pre-treats).

  There are a few stains, such as lipstick, mascara, and shoe polish, in which the dyes can be spread by water. These should be sponged with dry spotter before you get water anywhere near them. (See specific instructions under each particular stain.)

• **Presoak** problem items you come across, if indicated in the instructions for that stain.

• **Don't overload** your machine. All the detergent and pre-treat in the world can't get stains out (and clothes clean) if there isn't room for the agitator to do its thing—flush water thoroughly through the fabric.

• **Don't use hot water** unless the instructions for that stain specifically call for it (see p. 31).

• If the fabric will tolerate it, **use chlorine bleach.** It's much better at removing stains than the milder bleaches (but read the cautions first on pp. 32-34 and 56-58).

• After laundering, **check to see if the stain is still there**— then re-treat and wash again if necessary. Even if you think it's gone, air dry the item and take another look. Don't use any heat (such as hot-air drying or ironing) until you're sure it's 100 percent removed. Heat will set many stains and make them permanent.

• If this doesn't get it, try the specialized spot removers and techniques in "How to Go About It," then re-launder.

Detergent Strategy for Stainbusting

All laundry detergents do a superior job of removing everyday soil compared to the plain old soap we used to use, but in taking out stains, you'll probably notice a difference if you use the most effective products available. Liquid detergents such as Liquid

Cheer and Liquid Tide (both non-phosphates) are great for removing normal soil and especially good at keeping nylons white, but they don't remove makeup, ink, and oil stains as well as the powdered detergents, which are usually cheaper, too. Wisk is an excellent oil-stain remover, though it, too, doesn't whiten nylon as well. Enzyme detergents do a better job on protein stains such as grass, egg, blood, and gravy. For all-around soil removal, effectiveness on stains, and reasonable price, it's still hard to beat good old Tide, either the phosphate or non-phosphate formula. The phosphate formulas of Cheer and Oxydol are also very good, with the non-phosphate formulations of these products being a little less effective on stains, especially in cold water.

Laundry detergent contains surfactants and emulsifiers to lift off and wash away greasy soils, so pre-treating with laundry detergent (mixed into a paste with water, if it's the powdered type) or even laundering alone will remove some of the easier grease stains.

Water Temperature Wisdom

Without a doubt, detergents and bleaches work better in hot water than they do in cold. But when stain removing, we generally wash everything in warm. This gives the best possible cleaning action while avoiding heat-setting the stains. Only greasy stains are washed in hot, and only certain stains, such as blood and egg, are washed in cold. (See individual instructions for each stain in "How to Go About It.") A cold-water wash will also minimize shrinking if you're working with washable woolens, and avoid dye loss in very bright or dark colors.

For stain-removal laundering and for that matter any laundering, all rinses should be cold. It saves energy and reduces wrinkling, too.

To Bleach
or Not to Bleach

This is like trying to decide whether or not to draw a gun when you're cornered.

There are two types of bleaches commonly used for home laundry: liquid chlorine bleach, such as Clorox or Purex, and oxygen bleach, such as Clorox II or Snowy. Chlorine is unquestionably the better stain remover, but it's a powerful bleach that has to be used carefully to avoid fabric or color damage. Oxygen bleach is much milder and can be used safely on all washable fabrics, but it requires hot water to be of much use—it's only marginally effective in warm water and almost useless in cold. While chlorine bleach, too, does its best in hot water, it does an okay job in warm water and even fairly well in cold.

Repeated use of chlorine bleach in too strong a concentration on cotton and other natural fibers can weaken and deteriorate the fabric. Before you know it you'll be finding holes and faded colors in cotton and cotton-blend fabrics. But occasional use of chlorine bleach can work wonders in removing stubborn stains. If it isn't used too often and if it's diluted properly, it shouldn't harm bleach-safe fabrics.

Quick Henry, the Bleach!

Bleach isn't an only child, there's a whole family of bleaches. Here are the ones I recommend for stain removal, listed in order from strongest to weakest.

Chlorine bleach (sodium hypochlorite). Generally a liquid, such as Clorox or Purex. A good stain remover, but this is powerful stuff that has to be used with great care because it can damage skin and household surfaces (see pg. 32, 34).

Color remover. Designed to remove fabric dyes before re-dyeing, it can be a big help in getting rid of unwanted colors and dye stains, especially. But it too must be stored and handled cautiously (see p. 62).

Hydrogen peroxide. Yes, the same stuff we put on skinned knees can serve as a mild bleach that's safe for almost any fabric.

Oxygen or "all-fabric" bleach (sodium perborate). Available as both powder and liquid, this is a much milder bleach than chlorine and it needs hot water (which we don't often want to use in stain removal) to do its best work. It won't get as many of the spots out, but it's safer to use and safer for fabrics and surfaces. And can be used to make a paste for spot bleaching.

Lemon juice and vinegar. Are mild acids that have a mild safe bleaching action, as those freckle-fighting southern belles always knew.

Ammonia. Also has a mild bleaching action, useful on acid-sensitive fabrics such as cotton and linen.

Chlorine bleach is generally safe for all white or colorfast fabrics except wool, silk, mohair, fiberglass, and Spandex and certain flame-retardant finishes—check the label. The care labels required in garments manufactured since 1984 have to tell you whether you can use chlorine bleach.

> If in doubt, test first by mixing one tablespoon of chlorine bleach in one-quarter cup water. Put a drop of this solution on a hidden part of the object, leave it for a minute, and blot it out. If there's no color change, it's safe to bleach.

Always dilute liquid bleach according to directions, and be sure to measure accurately. Never put undiluted bleach directly on anything. Be sure to mix it in with the water before you add your laundry. Or use your washer's bleach dispenser. Chlorine bleach is very corrosive to metals and reacts strongly with acids and some alkalis to form poisonous chlorine gas, so you always need to be careful how and where you're using it. For stain removal on fabrics not safe for chlorine bleach, and for everyday laundry, use one of the safer oxygen (all-fabric) bleaches.

A Word about Fabric-Softener Spots

Fabric softeners coat the fibers of fabric with a lubricating film that helps them drape better, wrinkle less, feel softer, and attract less lint (by reducing static cling). This is all fine and desirable, but be sure to follow the drying temperature directions, especially for synthetics. The chemical in dryer sheets can leave oily spots on man-made fibers at high heat settings. The liquid fabric softeners you add to the rinse water can also leave spots if they're poured directly onto clothes. To remove these spots, sponge with water, rub in laundry detergent, and re-launder.

The Fine Points of Pre-treating

Pre-treats are the modern launderer's best friend. They can be found as pump and aerosol sprays, dispenser bottles, and laundry "sticks." Pre-treats contain soil dissolvers that penetrate stubborn stains and suspend them in the washwater so they can be flushed away. Some pre-treats also have enzymes or "active proteins" that break down protein stains such as blood, grass, milk, and egg.

The liquids (which includes the aerosols) do the best job of softening and removing tough stains, and they're usually pretty effective on greasy and oily spots. But you do have to be a little careful when you're using them. The solvents in some of them can damage paint (including the paint on washer and dryer tops!) and plastics, to say nothing of skin, eyes, and lungs. Liquid pre-treats should be applied just before you do the wash, and ideally be left on the spot or stain for just a minute or two before laundering. Less than a minute, and the pre-treat doesn't have enough time to penetrate the strain; more than a few minutes, and it can dry out. When this happens, the loosened soil which was held in suspension by the liquid pre-treat redeposits on the fibers, and may not come out in the wash.

When you're using a spray pre-treat, cover your work surface with a plastic sheet to avoid damage from overspray.

Try to avoid breathing the spray mist, and be sure to keep it out of your eyes!

The big drawback of liquid pre-treats is: We want to treat a stain when it's fresh, but we don't want to stop and wash the item right then. So we end up throwing it in the hamper untreated and waiting until we do a load of laundry to pre-treat. Some stains will set and become much harder to remove during that time.

The laundry sticks may be a little less powerful than the liquids, but they do have certain advantages. You can treat a stain immediately, then wait up to a week to wash. Some people keep a laundry stick by the clothes hamper and routinely "stick" any stains as they throw the dirty clothes in (what a great trick to teach your kids). The stick pre-treat won't dry out before your week is up, and the soil will still be softened, suspended, and ready to wash out when you get around to doing laundry. The sticks also pose less of a problem as far as ruining surfaces or getting in your lungs or eyes.

Different pre-treats have different formulas, and vary in how well they work on specific stains. Most of them will take out everyday grass, blood, food, and beverage stains, and oily stains like dressings and gravy. Some will take out one type of stain much better than another. Magic Wand is more effective on ink than most, for instance. For overall effectiveness on a wide range of stains, my favorite is liquid Shout. I don't like the aerosols as well as the pump sprays, because of the greater danger of breathing the finer aerosol mist.

Laundry pre-treats shouldn't be used for spot removal on carpeting, upholstery, dry-cleanable garments, or anything else that can't be laundered.

No matter what type of pre-treat you use: treat the whole spot, not just the middle or most of it. It wouldn't hurt to overlap a little onto the unspotted fabric beyond, especially for thick or aged spots. Work it in a little after you put it on; and bear in mind that some stains may need a second treating and a second laundering.

Stain Zones

These are the parts of our clothing especially prone to stains that need to be scanned every time we launder.

- **Ring around the . . .** Collars and cuffs (and hatbands, too) get hair and skin oil and, in the case of shirt cuffs, a lot of right-up-against-whatever-we're-working-on staining. Collars are a good place to check for shaving-cut blood specks, too.

• **The cuffs or hems** of light-colored pants, especially, are often smeared with mud, road tar, or shoe polish.

• **The fronts** (or "bib" sections) **of shirts and tops** are the scene of most of our food and drink fumbles. Look closely for overlooked spills and unnoticed stains. Clear soft-drink and fruit-juice dribbles are hard to see, for example. If not completely removed before ironing or hot-air drying, the sugar in stains like these can be heat-set and become permanent.

• **Underarms** and other sweat-soak spots.

• **Elbows** get a lot of lean-on and -into stains.

• **Knees** (ground-in soil and grass stains).

• **Seat.** As a professional cleaner of perching places I advise you to look closely at chairs and bus seats before you lower yourself into them. You'll be amazed what an assortment of gooey spots and sticky stains can be transferred from seats to our skirts and trousers. If in doubt as to origin, treat these as "mystery" stains (see p. 242-246).

Other hamper inhabitants worth casting a close eye over for stains: tablecloths, cloth napkins, sheets, pillowcases, mattress pads, underwear, and socks that have been worn without shoes!

A Dozen Good Ways to *Create* Stains in Laundry

1 Failing to sort the hamper contents into whites, dark colors, noncolorfast (quarantine) stuff, etc. Mother didn't make those piles for the fun of it.

2 Tossing the wrong thing in to "fill out a load" (you can never let your guard down on sorting).

---

3 Doing any laundry two hours before the trip, or in a great hurry.

---

4 Letting wet—or half-dry—clothes rest on top of each other for hours.

---

5 Pouring in bleach, especially liquid bleach, without letting the washer fill first.

---

6 Doing the wash while they're fixing the water system.

---

7 Using fabric-softener sheets in too hot a dryer.

---

8 Leaving laundry where the cat or dog can snuggle into it.

---

9 Ignoring the fact that the washer or dryer has a rusty drum.

---

10 Using mildewed or dirty clothespins.

---

11 Leaving the laundry on the line so long the birds bomb it.

---

12 Locating the clothesline under a mulberry tree.

Dye Transfer in Laundry: What Causes It and How to Cure It

Some dyes and fabrics get married and live happily ever after, but not a few of these unions end in divorce—or at least separation. When the dye bleeds out of a fabric in the washer, it's called "fugitive dye," and this is one fugitive that almost always gets caught, usually by your treasured white linen blouse or one-of-a-kind T-shirt. Of all the dyes, red is the least colorfast, with blue and purple next in line (in case you need a good excuse to wear green or brown). But any dark or bright color can bleed, and some fabrics tend to lose dye and pick up fugitive dye worse than others. Madras is notorious for dye bleeding, as are many silks and acetates, and nylon seems to have a knack for attracting whatever vagrant dye might be floating around.

Don't trust luck, hunches, or even labels when it comes to the question of how colorfast an item will be. The safest bet is to wash any new colored garment by itself until you get to know it. Never trust red garments in with other clothes—especially whites—even if they've been washed before. If you do get a "pink load" (or light blue, or lavender), don't dry it. Keep it wet. Rewash in warm water with chlorine bleach for white or colorfast fabrics, oxygen bleach for the rest. It may take several washings to completely remove the fugitive dye. If the color doesn't come out, you may have to use a color remover. Don't dry the load until the unwanted color is gone.

Yellowing

Yellowing can be caused by many things: White cotton and linen tend to yellow if stored in the dark for long periods. This kind of yellowing will usually come out with a hot-water wash in chlorine bleach. If you don't use enough detergent when you wash, or use too low a wash temperature, a gradual buildup of body oils will also yellow garments. A short or gentle wash cycle may also not be enough to remove all the soil from heavily soiled laundry. This condition can usually be reversed by presoaking in a bleach/enzyme product such as Biz and washing with hot water and chlorine bleach, if safe for the fabric. Color remover can be used on white fabrics that can't take bleach.

Another cause of yellowing is chlorine retention in bleach-sensitive fibers such as Spandex, silk, wool, and resin-finished fabrics. Try a color remover, but this condition often can't be reversed. Another irreversible type of yellowing is the kind caused by hanging whites with light-sensitive brighteners out in the sun to dry. If the care label says "dry out of direct light" it means what it says. A garment with yellowed fabric brightener is never going to be sparkling white again.

Iron or manganese in the water supply can also cause yellow or brown stains on white fabrics. See p. 263-265 for how to remove these.

Stain Removal Strategy When Laundering

- Stay alert for stains—before you wash, dry, or iron.

- Wash it **now**—the sooner you get to it, the better your chances of washing it away.

- Don't pop it in the washer until you've brushed or scraped all of the stain you can away.

- Pre-treat! (And wash the object shortly thereafter if using a liquid pre-treat.)

- Presoak if Part III of the book tells you to.

- Use **warm** water unless Part III tells you otherwise.

- Use chlorine bleach if safe for the fabric.

- Don't overload the machine!

3 THE OLD

STANDBYS

(From Club Soda to Toothpaste to Meat Tenderizer)

If you've ever tried to cut something with a dull knife, I'm sure you ended up with some ragged edges. But you may have managed to get the job done—it was better than nothing. That's how I classify many of the hints and tips in newspapers, books, and magazines—the home remedies for stain removal. These old wives' and old husbands' tales have been around a long time— and some for good reason. A few of them work pretty well. Vinegar and alcohol for example, are staples even in the pro spotter's kit. Others work, but not as reliably or well as widely available and inexpensive professional stain-removal products. Not a few of the home brews, though they do remove stains, have side effects that only cause new problems—there are better, safer alternatives. In a pinch a home remedy might be worth using if nothing else is at hand, but only if you pay strict attention to certain precautions. All the rest, sad to say, are a waste of time and energy on your part. Let's take a look at all these to see which are worthwhile and which to steer clear of, before getting into the serious business of stain removing.

What It Is and What's in It	What It Does	Comments
Club soda Carbonated water, citric acid	Acts as a very mild acid cleaner—slightly more effective than plain water for water-soluble stains	Save your money—vinegar-and-water is cheaper
Denture cleaning tablets Oxygen bleach—perborate)	Will take coffee, tea, and juice stains out of teacups	So will vinegar and most other bleaches
Hair spray Alcohol and other volatile solvents and resins	Dissolves ink (the cheaper brands of hair spray are better for this purpose)	Must be removed (laundered) afterward or will stiffen fabric—okay to use as a laundry pre-treat for ink stains
Fingernail polish remover Amyl acetate, maybe acetone, maybe oils	Will dissolve fingernail polish, and possibly airplane glue	Oily types will leave a stain—and you don't ever want to use acetone on acetate fabrics
Cola Phosphoric acid, sugar, coloring, and carbonated water	Acts as a mild acid cleaner for things like toilet bowls and whitewall tires	Not as effective as a regular phosphoric acid cleaner—and the sugar and caramel coloring in cola create stain problems of their own
Ashes Cigarette or cigar ashes, sometimes mixed with fats or oils	Combined with fats, ashes form a mild soap, which is also mildly abrasive, used to rub water rings off furniture	Ashes also contain carbon, which will cause its own stains—better to use rottenstone (available in paint stores and furniture finishing departments) or another clean abrasive on porous surfaces

What It Is and What's in It	What It Does	Comments
Toothpaste Mild soap, with flavoring and abrasives	Acts as mild abrasive cleaner	But it's messier to use than a lot of other abrasives. And like any abrasive it can leave surfaces dull and scratched. So use it sparingly and gently and make sure it's the plain white kind

Peanut butter Peanuts, vegetable oil	The oil in peanut butter softens and lubricates hardened stains, such as chewing gum. And because peanut butter is pasty it can be applied almost like a poultice	Leaves an oil stain of its own which must be removed
Meat tenderizer Contains enzymes, possibly spices, salt, coloring	The enzymes "digest" protein stains such as meat juices, eggs, blood, milk	Not as effective as pure enzymes, and the other ingredients may create problems
Salt Sodium chloride	Helpful in absorbing potentially damaging stains such as red wine and Kool-Aid	But it must be applied immediately, then brushed and rinsed away when dry

What It Is and What's in It	What It Does	Comments
Cutter insect repellent "Deet" (N, N-diethyl-meta-toluamide)—a penetrating, oily solvent	Will dissolve ink and some oil-based stains	Damages Spandex, rayon, acetate, plastics, vinyl, paint—test before using
Alcohol A powerful solvent—useful in removing many types of dye stains	Can also make fabric dyes run—particularly in silk and acetate—test before using	For stain removal you want to use denatured or isopropyl, not rubbing alcohol, which may contain perfume or excess water
TSP Trisodium phosphate	A strong alkaline detergent booster or "builder." Helps break down fatty and oily soils	A solution as alkaline as this will set some stains, such as tannin, tumeric, and sugar; safer to use a neutral detergent (see p. 59) or dry spotter (see p. 58-59) on oily stains.
Lemon juice Citric acid	A mild bleach, useful in removing wine, rust, and other stains	Test first before using on silk, wool, cotton, linen, rayon, or acetate
Baking soda Sodium bicarbonate	Neutralizes acid stains (such as bowl cleaner stains) and acid solutions, absorbs odors, acts as a mild bleach, and mixed with water into a paste, serves as a mild abrasive cleanser	Rinse away powder after using and bear in mind that vigorous scrubbing with baking soda may dull glossy surfaces

What It Is and What's in It	What It Does	Comments
Vinegar Acetic acid	Neutralizes alkaline stains and spotter residues, also acts as a mild bleach. Useful in many stain-removal operations	Use **white** vinegar only for stain removing and dilute with two parts water for use on cotton or linen; pretest for dye change before using on colored fabrics
Soap Real soap, such as Ivory Snow, Lux, Woolite, and most bath bars, as opposed to detergent	Helpful in removing many types of stains— penetrates and lifts soil and lubricates the cleaning process	Don't use soap on fruit stains—it will set them. And for stain removal you don't want a soap with strong colorings, scents, skin conditioners, deodorizers, or other ingredients not 100 percent helpful to the stain-removal process
Shaving cream Mild soap, glycerin, skin conditioners	About as effective as real soap, but messier	Forget it, unless squirting it out of the can gives you a thrill

4 YOUR

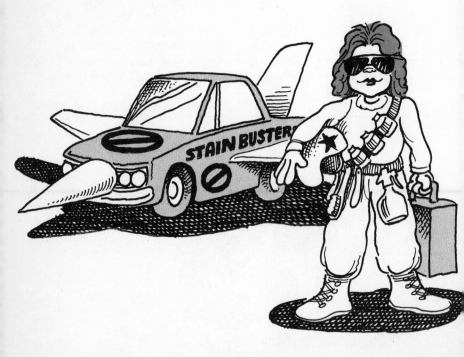

STAIN-BUSTING KIT

(The Tools of the Trade)

Don't let this list of spotting tools and chemicals scare you off—you can jump in at whatever level you want. There may be a couple dozen things here, but only a few of them are new to you, and I'd bet you have ten of them on the premises already! (It's enough to make a stain shrink in horror.) Here's the key:

***Must-haves.** You need these for even a bare bones spotting kit. Assemble what you already have on hand, then go out and get the rest and you'll be all set to start stainbusting.

Welcome additions. These will round out your kit and give you what you need to handle most common stains.

*The ultimate.** With just these six things more, you'll be outfitted like a pro. Even the tough and exotic stains are within your reach.

Don't be buffaloed by the idea of stopping by the pharmacist and picking up some "amyl acetate" or "acetone," either. We spend weeks, if not months, of our life battling the damage and embarrassment of stains—a few minutes and a couple of dollars getting the right stuff will go a long way toward changing that. Think of the time and money we spend for complexion blemish removal—the blotches on our clothes, floors, and furniture are almost as noticeable.

Why can't I just use a miracle all-in-one spot remover?

We see ads all the time for miracle stain-removing sticks, liquids, sprays, and powders. They promise to remove virtually any stain like magic, or your money back. Most of them do fine on a certain range of stains, but none of them is good at everything. Different types of stains call for different cleaning chemistry, and no one product can do it all. If you find one that works unusually well on a particular type of stain, add it to your spotting kit. Keep the packaging and directions with the product so you have all the info when you need it. But don't expect one chemical to handle every stain you get.

Tools

***Scraper.** Many spot-getting procedures in this book call for scraping. Professional spotters use a "bone scraper" or spatula, which is made of bone, plastic, or metal. You can get one at a janitorial-supply store or dry cleaners' supplier. Janitorial-supply stores can be found in the Yellow Pages under that very heading. But for home use, a butter knife works just fine—use the blade for scraping, and the handle for gentle agitation (see p. 76-77). Keep one in your spotting kit that has a simple, straight handle and a smooth, dull blade (no nicks or serrations). For fabrics you wouldn't want to scrape with even as blunt a blade as this, you can use the bowl of a soup spoon. (For scraping technique, see p. 70-71.)

***Clean white cloths.** You want **white** cloths for stain removal. Spotting chemicals can cause dyed fabrics to bleed or transfer color, and white cloths allow you to keep a close eye out for this. They also enable you to keep track of how much stain is coming out and when it stops coming out.

Your stain kit cloths need not only to be white, but **absor-bent**—and you'd be amazed how many inhabitants of the rag bag aren't. For absorbency, you want cotton—which means cotton terrycloth, cotton T-shirts, cotton diapers, or one of Don Aslett's famous cleaning cloths (an eighteen-inch by eighteen-inch square of terrycloth, hemmed, folded over once and stitched together into a "tube," then folded up into a size to fit the task at hand). Old white linen napkins are good and absorbent, too. For many of the stain-removal procedures in this book you'll want to fold your cloth into a pad about the size of your hand and about a quarter to half an inch thick. A terry hand towel folded to washcloth size fits this description nicely.

***Spray bottle.** A plastic bottle with a "trigger sprayer" like you'd use for misting houseplants or spray cleaning. In stain removal we use this mainly for flushing, and if you like you can just use a plastic squeeze bottle instead.

**Spotting brush. A professional spotting brush has short, closely set bristles for "tamping" stains (see p. 76-77 for an explanation of this) and a scraper on the end of the handle. You can use any small brush that has not-too-long bristles all the same length—odd bristles poking out anywhere are likely to damage the fabric. The brush you use on lightweight fabrics shouldn't be as stiff as a spotting brush for carpet or upholstery. A soft or medium toothbrush works fine for small stains on garments, but you'll want a larger brush for carpet stains and heavier use. The flat-faced kind used to put on shoe polish works pretty well, as long as it's never been used to put on shoe

Am Ex, etc.—Don't leave home without it

We're out somewhere and "splat"—a hunk of gooey gravy-soaked mashed potatoes falls on our lap. Our first reaction is a glance to see if our fine balancing act was noticed. Then we want to do something, because we know if we leave a mess on our lap or the carpet or car seat, it sets; if we try rubbing it away it will only penetrate deeper and spread farther. To remove it, we have on hand the tiniest and finest scraper and dustpan around—a firm, water-proof, germproof credit card. With it you can scoop up goop, stain, and even broken glass. I've fielded spilled trays in a second while an alarmed busboy searched for a broom. Credit cards are a cinch to clean off afterward, too!

polish. If you want a genuine spotting brush, most janitorial-supply stores have them.

**Nylon scrub pad. Does a better and safer job than a brush when scrubbing action is really needed, such as on hard surfaces. Available as plain nylon pads (such as Scotch-Brite) or nylon-faced sponges, in either form it's the safe-for-all-surfaces white nylon type you want, not a green or brown one.

A stainbuster knows that tools and working areas need to be clean, too. It's not going to help a bit to have the remains of last month's shrimp creole catastrophe still stuck to the roots of our spotting brush when we go to tidy up the corner behind the chair where Mitzie had her six pups. Rinse brushes vigorously after use and hang to dry. When you use your tools on sticky stuff like nail polish or glue, wipe it off before it cements itself on there.

Keep your absorbing cloths nice and clean (they don't have to be snowy white, but **clean**) and dryer drying them will help keep them soft and thirsty. And retire them when they get rank and stiff with stain.

Chemicals

***Ammonia. Some stains require a slightly alkaline spotting agent. We add a few drops of ammonia to our wet spotter to make it alkaline where needed, and also use it to neutralize certain acid stains and spotting chemicals. Ammonia can also serve as a mild bleach. Get plain household ammonia, not the sudsy or lemon type, at the supermarket. Always pretest before using ammonia, as it affects some dyes. If you note a color change when using it, rinse with water, apply a few drops of white vinegar to neutralize the ammonia, then rinse again. Don't use ammonia on silk or wool unless absolutely necessary, and then only diluted with an equal amount of water. Where directions call for a mild solution, use one tablespoon of ammonia in one-half cup of water. Don't inhale the fumes—we've all had at least one experience of taking a big deep sniff of ammonia—your nostrils don't need to go through it again. And don't get ammonia on your skin or in your eyes!

***Chlorine bleach.** Liquid bleach, such as Clorox or Purex. This is sodium hypochlorite, a potent bleach not recommended for everyday laundry because it tends to weaken natural fabrics such as cotton, but it can be a big help in stain removal. Don't ever use it on silk, wool, Spandex, fiberglass, or on permanent press fabrics or those treated with flame-retardant resins. Always pretest chlorine bleach before using, and be careful not to breathe the fumes or get it in your eyes or on your skin. Don't use metal spoons or containers with liquid chlorine bleach, and never mix it with any other cleaning chemical. Don't use it straight—dilute it with at least four parts water for stain removal on sturdy fabrics, eight parts water for more delicate fabrics. Always rinse it out of the fabric right after you use it. Watch closely for color change and rinse immediately if you see any sign of a dye change. If possible, bleach the entire garment, not just the spot, to avoid uneven color change.

***Hydrogen peroxide.** A mild bleach safe for all fabrics. Effective on a surprising number of stains, especially blood and scorch. Pretest before using on colored fabrics. Get the 3 percent solution sold in drugstores as an antiseptic, not the stronger solution used for bleaching hair. Use it straight from the bottle without diluting. Don't buy too much, as it loses strength when stored for long periods. Adding a few drops of ammonia accelerates the bleaching action of peroxide.

***Synthetic bleaches.** All-fabric oxygen bleaches, such as Clorox II and Snowy, are safe for all colorfast fabrics, and can be used in laundry or mixed with water to form a paste for spot bleaching. Not nearly as effective as chlorine bleach at removing stains.

***Digestant.** A product containing enzymes that actually digest stubborn protein stains (meat juice, egg, blood, milk). Digestants are available as pure enzymes from druggists (**pepsin** or **papain** for proteins, **amylase** for starch and carbohydrates) or as combination bleach/enzyme laundry aids such as Biz and Axion. Digestants can be used as laundry pre-soaks or as pastes for spotting dry cleanables. Warm water makes them work better. For soaking almost anything except bloodstains, mix the digestant in warm water according to label directions and soak for 30 minutes to an hour. To make a paste, mix equal parts powder and water, and pretest for colorfastness before using (if it's a bleach product, follow label directions for color testing). Leave the paste on the spot for 15 to 30 minutes, but don't let it dry out. Rinse thoroughly. Don't use digestants on wool or silk.

***Dry spotter.** A "dry" (solvent-based) spot remover, as opposed to a "wet" (water-based) spotter. Effective in removing oily and greasy stains, especially from water-sensitive fabrics. Dry spotters can be used on virtually any fabric without damage, and will not set stains. (But it never hurts to pretest first.) If in doubt about the nature of a stain, it's safest to start out with a dry spotter, before using any water.

Dry spotters are available in supermarkets and variety stores as products such as Energine, Carbona, Afta, or K2r (a solvent spotter in powder form that you spray on and brush off after it dries). Most janitorial-supply stores also carry handy ready-to-use liquid and aerosol solvent spotters. Dry spotters shouldn't be used on wet fabric—always allow it to dry first.

Use sparingly on upholstery and carpet, as solvents deteriorate the foam used in upholstery cushions and the latex adhesives used to glue carpeting together. Always use them in a well-ventilated place and don't use them on clothing that you haven't taken off yet. And keep out of reach of children!

***Laundry pre-treat.** Can help to remove a great many spots just in the course of ordinary laundering, especially greasy spots. Pre-treats are put on and allowed to soak a few minutes before washing. Examples are Shout, Spray 'n Wash, and Magic Pre-Wash. Pre-treats need to be rinsed out or laundered after use, and shouldn't be allowed to dry on the fabric. You also don't want to get them in your eyes, or on paint or plastic. (For more on pre-treats see Chapter 2.)

***Neutral detergent.** When a stain-removal instruction calls for this, use a liquid hand-dishwashing detergent such as Joy. Don't use an opaque or colored one, which may contain skin conditioners or dye—you want a clear one. Don't ever use heavy-duty household cleaners, automatic dishwashing compounds, or laundry detergents—they're too alkaline, and can set some stains.

***Vinegar.** A mild (5 percent) solution of acetic acid, vinegar is used on stains that call for an acid spotter. It's also used to neutralize some alkaline stains and spotting chemicals, and can even serve as a mild bleach. Vinegar is especially useful on silk and wool, neither of which tolerate ammonia well. Avoid using it on cotton and linen. Don't use on acetate. Use only **white** vinegar, not the colored wine or cider types. When directions call for a mild solution, mix 1:4 with water. Vinegar may cause color change in some dyes. If color change occurs, rinse well with water, add a few drops of ammonia, then rinse again.

***Water.** The great cleaning medium; most spotting procedures call for water at some point. Unless otherwise specified, this means room-temperature water. Water must be used sparingly on fabrics such as silk and rayon, which tend to water-spot, and on 100 percent wool.

If you have hard water you might want to use soft or distilled water for spotting, because the dissolved minerals in hard water not only interfere with the action of soaps and detergents, but leave whitish stains of their own. (As anyone who's tried to just hose the dust off a car knows!)

***Wet spotter.** All-purpose spotter, which is effective on most water-based stains. This is usually a mixture of detergents, solvents, and surfactants (chemicals that make water wetter so it penetrates better and faster). All-purpose spotters are available in supermarkets, variety and janitorial-supply stores. They usually come in handy plastic squeeze bottles that help you put just the right amount of chemical on the stain. The best one I've found is one of the newer ones. Unbelievable Stain Remover from Core Products of Irving, Texas. Chemspec Spot Lifter and Whink Carpet Stain Remover are good, too. Wet spotters should be okay on any water-safe colorfast fabric, but always pretest to be sure. If you have a stain emergency and no wet spotter, use laundry pre-treat, but always rinse it out with water afterward.

**Absorbent. A granular or sawdust-like material used for blotting or soaking up fresh stains, especially grease and oil. Use kitty litter for heavy stains like oil drips in the garage, cornmeal on light-colored fabrics, fuller's earth (available at pharmacies) on dark-colored fabrics. Cornstarch and talcum powder work too, but can be hard to remove from fabric. If left on long enough (several hours to all day), absorbents can often remove an oil stain completely. Rub it in and let it sit a while, then brush or vacuum off.

Keeping the Scene of the Grime from Becoming the Scene of the Crime

When mechanics work on our car, our biggest complaint is often not the work they do or even the bill they deliver, but the grease, dirt, and damage on the car seat, floor, door handle, hood, steering wheel, and so on. All because they didn't protect it from their fixing fallout! How many times in your life (when trying to fix or clean something—or remove a stain from it) have you inflicted more stain or damage on it than it had to begin with? Such as when you try to take the fingernail polish off the tabletop, and remove the varnish instead.

Removing stains involves chemicals and moisture, and in the process of pulling it out, we always push some of it through. And there's usually another stainable—carpet, flooring, wall, or underwear—waiting right behind or below to absorb the just-released problem. Such as when you use a solvent to remove a spot from your Levi's while your legs are still in them, and the solvent seeps through to your skin to give you an ugly rash.

You can't always slide a piece of glass or wood (the best things for the purpose) under something when you're taking out a spot, but on almost anything from a bedspread to a tablecloth you can slip an absorbent towel or like protector between your working area and the nearest surface.

Alcohol. A powerful solvent that's especially useful for fabrics you can't use water on. For stain removal you want either denatured or isopropyl alcohol—both of these are available at drugstores. Denatured is best for "dry clean only" fabrics, as it contains less water. Don't use rubbing alcohol, which may contain perfumes and dyes as well as excessive water. **CAUTION: Alcohol can make dyes run, especially in silk and acetates, so always pretest in an inconspicuous place. When using alcohol on acetates, always dilute it with two parts water. Alcohol is also extremely flammable, so don't use it around sparks or flame.

Color remover. Designed to remove the **old color before re-dyeing fabrics, color removers do indeed remove many dyes from white fabrics. Some desperate and courageous cleaners use color removers successfully on colorfast dyed fabrics, too, but it's tricky. Color remover can sometimes cause a radical color change in colored fabric (such as from green to orange!). And if that happens you may be able to return things to normal by rinsing immediately with water. Colors simply faded or bleached by color remover, on the other hand, can't be restored. Rit Color Remover, available at supermarkets and variety stores, is a good one. **Poisonous:** Always use strictly according to label directions.

**Glycerin. Available at pharmacies, glycerin is used to soften and dissolve hardened stains. Particularly helpful on wool and other water-sensitive fabrics.

**Soap. When stain-removal procedures call for soap, use a mild true soap such as Ivory Snow laundry soap or Woolite. Bar soap such as Ivory or Lux is okay, but for stain removal don't use bar soaps that contain coloring, skin conditioners, or deodorants. And don't use soap on stains unless the instructions specifically tell you to—it sets some stains, such as fruit!

Outright pet odor eliminator. A bacteria/enzyme digester that eliminates organic waste by **eating it. It's a live culture of friendly bacteria that keep reproducing and producing enzymes that digest the waste until it's all gone. About the only way to completely remove pet stains from carpet and upholstery. Follow label directions, and bear in mind that bacteria/enzyme digesters always take time to work, because the little enzyme bugs take such tiny bites. (Should not be used on wool or silk.) Available in pet stores and janitorial-supply stores.

**Petroleum jelly. White petrolatum, such as Vaseline. Used to soften and break up hardened grease and oil stains.

*Acetone. A special solvent helpful in removing paint, fingernail polish, airplane glue, and lacquer. Available at paint stores and hobby shops. Never use acetone on acetate, triacetate, or modacrylic, or you'll end up with some extra buttonholes—acetone melts and dissolves fabrics like these. You also have to use it with care on rayon, silk, or wool. It should be safe for most other fabrics, but always pretest to be sure. Acetone is very flammable and gives off **poisonous** fumes, so always work with it in a well-ventilated place and never around sparks or flame. Protect your work surface, too, because it can damage furniture finishes and plastics.

*Amyl acetate (banana oil). Can safely remove fingernail polish, lacquer, and model airplane glue from acetates and other fabrics that would be damaged by acetone. Get the chemically pure kind, available at pharmacies. Protect your work surface when using it, because it too can **damage furniture finishes and plastic.**

*De-Solve-it. A citrus oil product especially good for dissolving adhesives and gum. Sold in supermarkets and hardware and janitorial-supply stores. Must be removed by laundering or with a dry spotter after use to avoid leaving an oil stain.

*Oxalic acid. Useful in removing rust and some kinds of ink stains. Available in crystal (powdered) form at drug and hardware stores, it can be used as a solution (one tablespoon crystals to one cup warm water), or as a paste. **Poisonous:** Observe all label precautions.

*Gum Freeze. An aerosol specifically designed to unstick the ickies (see p. 72, 74). Available at janitorial-supply stores.

Must-Haves for the Stainbuster's Kit

Scraper

Clean white cotton cloths

Spray bottle or
  squeeze bottle

Plain household ammonia

Chlorine bleach

Three percent hydrogen
  peroxide

All-fabric bleach such as
  Chlorox II or Snowy

Digestant

Dry spotter

Laundry pre-treat

Neutral detergent

White vinegar

Wet spotter

Excellent Additions to Any Stain Kit

Spotting brush

Nylon scrub pad

Absorbent such as kitty litter or fuller's earth

Denatured or isopropyl alcohol

Color remover

Glycerin

Outright Pet Odor Eliminator

Petroleum jelly

Soap such as Ivory Snow or Woolite

A medium-stiff brush for dry brushing

Distilled water, if you have very hard water

Add These for the Ultimate Stain Kit

Acetone

Amyl acetate

De-Solve-it (citrus oil dissolvant)

Oxalic acid

A dry sponge and/or art gum eraser

An aerosol can of gum freeze

5

THE ABC's OF STAIN-BUSTING

(The Tricks of the Trade)

If I told you tennis, photography, playing the piano, or something else you really wanted to learn had forty or fifty basic principles involved you'd flinch, but you would probably still tackle them. Well, stain removal really only has three, and you can learn them just by watching. You can pull up a chair in front of any washing machine and watch—and you'll know all the basics of smart, efficient spot removal.

Chemical action is the soap, solvent, or other chemical we use to cut the smut—to dissolve the stain stuff and get it in solution (floating in the water). It's the laundry detergent, in the case of our friend the washer.

Mechanical action is the movement involved—blotting, brushing, scraping, or agitation—a special technique we'll learn for stainbusting—that helps the chemicals do their job. It breaks up and removes the bulk of the mess so they **can** do it. And it helps work the chemicals in so they can work faster and better. In your washing machine, it's the agitator.

Flushing or rinsing with water or solvent then carries the stain stuff away just like a silt-laden stream spirits off our topsoil.

Yes . . . Spot and stain removal is that simple!

And you can make it even simpler by practicing the famous executive management move called delegation. You can use your smarts to get someone else to do most of the work—and as I explained in Chapter 3, I mean the washing machine—you can feed the washer most of your problems. The washer, used with a bit of timing and prudence, will get three of every four stains out of your life.

The specialized stainbusting techniques that follow come into play when you're working on dry-cleanable garments, delicate washables, carpet, upholstery, and other things you can't throw in the washer, and for stains that don't respond to laundering. And when any stain-removal process is all through, it's always a good idea to launder washable items afterward to make sure the spotting chemicals are 100 percent removed.

TIMING

Stain Removal's Biggest Secret!

Stains and spots are just like cement—the longer you wait, the harder it gets!

Now (on)	**Tonight (in)**	**Tomorrow (set!)**
The time to act for an easy out.	By now the stain's had a chance to sink and settle in!	Now it's going to take lots of time, sweat, and chemicals (**if** you can even get it out).

The Basic
Stainbusting Techniques

Blot. Liquids just love to go to a dry place, so give 'em a chance. Blotting is simply applying something absorbent to slurp up the stain—blotting a spill while it's still wet is a hundred times more effective than trying to muscle it up after it's dry. Good quick blotting will take care of a lot of spills—and if you don't soak 'em up, believe me, whatever they're spilled on will! And then you'll pay the price to get them out!

For fresh liquid spills, blotting is usually the first step—to remove as much free liquid as possible before applying any kind of stain remover. On carpets and upholstery, where flushing and rinsing aren't possible, blotting comes into play again. We apply a chemical, let it work, and then blot it back out. Unless otherwise specified, always blot with a clean white cotton cloth (see p. 53-54).

When finishing up carpet stain removal, it's always a good idea, too, to blot to prevent stains from doing their magical reappearing act (see p. 145-146).

Scrape. Scraping spots always makes me think of that rascally rubber flipper someone invented to squeegee the frosting or other bowls so clean nothing was left for us kids to lick up. A flat surface like this used gently can indeed scoop up every bit of something. In spot removal, scraping is used both to remove loose material from the surface and to work chemical spotters into a stain. For either operation, the scraper should be held relatively flat against the surface and worked back and forth with a sliding motion. You aren't skinning a buffalo, so don't use the edge or point of the scraper to "dig" or gouge a stain—this will almost surely damage the fabric. Use special care when scraping delicate or loosely woven fabrics, or acetate, which marks easily. Use patience and light pressure, sliding the scraper back and forth gently to break up crusty stains, and to work the spotter into the fabric. As the spotter loosens the stain, the scraper removes the softened material, opening up the next layer below to the action of the chemical.

Dry-brush. This is the only brushing you ever want to do in stain removal: a light brushing with a medium-stiff brush to get rid of dry, caked-on spots such as mud. Just remember that you want to knock it loose, not scrub it deeper into the fiber. So use a gentle lifting motion to flick the particles up and away from the surface and use a vacuum to get the rest. Fine powders such as flour, face powder, or copy machine toner should be vacuumed in any case.

Always dry-brush and vacuum before working on a dry carpet or upholstery stain, to break loose and remove as much dry soil as you can. We also dry-bush to remove powdered spot removers such as K2r, or dried poultices (see p. 78-79). The only way we use a brush during the "wet" part of spotting is in tamping or light pounding to agitate the fibers (see p. 76-77), never to scrub. Scrubbing a spot only causes it to spread, and you "fur" the fibers, so before you know it your carpet or cardigan has an Afro.

Freeze. Remember the news story about the man in Alaska (it was sixty below that morning) who hit his spare tire with a hammer and it shattered? That gives you an idea of freeze power, and it's by far the best way to remove gobs of gum, tar, or candle wax, which only get messier when softened with a solvent.

A can of aerosol chewing gum remover from a janitorial-supply store freezes gooey deposits faster and harder than anything. Spray a stream on the goo for a few seconds—enough to freeze it hard. Then immediately (before it has a chance to warm up and soften again) give it a few good whacks with the handle of your butter knife to fracture the brittle mass. Quickly

Right after you drop it

You were watching the poor food selection of another customer (instead of your own) and crash! You push your tray right off the end of the rail, and everyone in the room gets a close look at what *you* picked as it dynamically displays itself all over the floor. Biscuits roll twenty feet away and come to rest right under the most beautiful person's chair. The drink splashes three feet up the legs of the nearby table and all over the next customer in line. The peas, like wild green BBs, sprinkle the cafeteria offerings colorfully, but not nearly as colorfully as your fall, which bazookaed barbecued pork all the way down the food line.

It's unquestionably one of life's most embarrassing moments. You've done it in supermarkets too, pulled a bottle of juice off the shelf and had it crash to the floor—and you've knocked over your cup or glass at the table any number of times. I once tried to cut frozen butter; it squirted ike a torpedo across the living-room rug at an elegant sugar-plantation dinner.

Accidents like this are like a public announcement: "Boy, look at the klutz," and our face is not just red but stained with what we fell on.

It's bound to happen again, so remember the onlookers always feel more uncomfortable than you. The minute you take control of the spill you've won! Take full responsibility for it, and you'll have everyone on your side with awe and respect.

Act quickly and even dramatize a little if necessary to keep the mess from hurting anyone or anything. Come up with a joke: "Hey, folks, the last one I spilled was on my boss's lap." Quickly take out a credit card and scoop and scrape the remains onto the tray or plate. It'll amaze you how fast and easy it is, and it'll impress the crowd so much they'll clap for you. Lay napkins in the liquid to absorb it quickly, and even when the owner finally arrives and waves you away, remain helpful—it works every time. Your ineptitude turns into an opportunity to be congratulated, and you might even get a free meal out of it! Never run—things like broken glass could cause problems injurious to far more than pride. Just be careful cleaning the stuff off people's legs or laps—black eyes don't match red faces!

scrape back and forth to break it up further into crumbs and make them "powder" off. Then brush or vacuum away the crumbs quick, or they'll just re-adhere as soon as they soften.

Most spots of this type are in carpeting, which will tolerate a fairly heavy-handed attack if you make sure the knife blade is dull and smooth, with no nicks or serrations to snag fibers. On a delicate fabric, just pluck and scrape the crumbs away with your fingernail.

Dry ice (available at ice cream equipment dealers, locker plants, and even some supermarkets) can also be used to freeze stains. It's colder than water ice, less messy, and safer to use on fabrics that can't stand water. If you use ordinary ice cubes on a water-sensitive fabric, put them in a well-sealed plastic bag. Small gummed-up items can just be stuck in the freezer.

Soak. Like your washer, soaking can do a lot of the work for you, and soaking is free! Soaking was the rule for any rusted or stubborn parts on the farm where I grew up. Instead of attacking the item with chisels and hammers, instead of beating or prying it to death, we sprayed it with a solvent and left it! After the solvent worked on the rust a while the offending part would almost fall off by itself.

Patience is a virtue in many things, but especially in stain removal. A chemical or liquid often needs to sit on the surface awhile to penetrate and soften a stain. You want to soak for at least 30 minutes, and longer periods (up to overnight for sturdy fabrics) will often be more effective. Don't overdo it with colored fabrics, though—some dyes will run when soaked too long.

When the directions call for soaking a washable item, just immerse it (or the stained part) in a pan or container filled with the solution. We soak dry cleanables, carpet, and upholstery by folding a clean white cotton cloth into a pad, dampening it with the solution, and applying it to the stained area. Don't use too big a pad or get it too wet—you want to keep the liquid confined to the area of the stain, not let it spread all over. You may have to re-dampen the pad occasionally to keep it from drying out.

A Sharp Eye for All the Pie

Our new house was almost finished, and we moved in just hours before my wife and newest daughter were due home from the hospital. When picking-up time came I still had the side-entrance double doors to hang. Deciding to do that later, I left and brought mom and the new baby home. One hour was long enough for the biggest of all milk cows to walk into the living room and drop the most enormous cow-pie you can imagine.

I cleaned it off the newly laid cork tile floor quick, but it wasn't until reading time, painting time, dusting time, and moving time later that I realized the great green stain wasn't the whole story. As time went by I found splatters on the wall, on the library books, under the piano, on top of pictures, even on the pencil sharpener.

Let that be a lesson to you about stains. We often don't realize that it hit our collar, tie, and belt before it came to rest on our thigh.

Stains get around—they bounce, seep, splash, run, wick mysteriously, and hide, even in the very thing you're cleaning. Never assume that the big one is the only one! Stop, and look around. The mechanic doesn't just repair what you say, he checks out the rest of the car too, just in case!

Sponge. A sponge may be what we call our worthless brother-in-law who manages to get something out of everybody, but it's also the most called-for technique for applying spotter to stains. (And amazingly enough there's no sponge involved!) To "sponge" you put down a pad of folded clean white absorbent cloth and lay the stained article on it, face down if possible. Use another clean cloth pad to apply the spotting chemical to the back of the stain. Work from the outside of the stain toward the center to avoid spreading it, and keep the damp area as small as possible by using short, light strokes and as little liquid as possible.

Use the cloth pad like a sponge to "push" the spotting solution through the fabric, and as you work the spotter through change the pad underneath as often as necessary to keep it dry and clean enough to check for color (stain or dye) transfer. Keep on sponging until no more color is being transferred. Change the sponging pad, too, as it picks up color, to keep from spreading the stain.

Tamp. The professional term for the right way to use a spotting brush, which is never to rub or scrub, but to **agitate** the stain.

As I said earlier, we usually need some kind of physical action to help dislodge the soil from a surface so it can be removed. But instead of dragging a brush across the surface as we do in scrubbing (not all that effective, as well as risking damage to delicate surfaces), tamping "agitates"—jiggles and jostles—just the area of the stain itself, to help break all the stain matter free. To tamp, spread the stained fabric out face up on a hard, smooth, level surface like a good thick piece of glass or the porcelain top of the washer or dryer. Strike the stain lightly but squarely with the flat face of a spotting brush (see p. 76 for exactly what kind that is). Be careful not to hit with the hard corner of the brush or the edge of the bristles—this could distort or damage the fabric or even chip the porcelain. Use only as much force as the fabric will tolerate. Tightly woven, durable fabrics and carpeting can withstand fairly forceful tamping, while loosely woven or delicate fabrics call for a gentler touch. You're not trying to beat it to death, just to strike hard enough with the ends of the bristles to break up the crust of the stain and work the spotting agent into it. Even if the instructions don't specifically call for it, you can tamp any time you need to, to loosen residue or help the spotter penetrate.

Flush. Flushing means applying liquid lavishly enough that it flows through the fabric and washes out whatever it is we're trying to remove—the stain itself or the spotting chemical we just used. Flushing can be done with a squeeze bottle, spray bottle, or even an eyedropper. Flush from the back side of the fabric whenever possible, so the stain is washed back out the way it came in, instead of being forced deeper. Put an absorbent cloth pad on the face of the spot, and apply the liquid through the back no faster than the pad can absorb it, to avoid enlarging the wet area. Change the pad as needed.

On carpets and upholstery, we flush by sponging the liquid on and blotting it back out with a clean towel.

For some stains, as noted under the individual stain removal instructions, we flush by rapidly running water through the fabric under a faucet, or pouring boiling water through it to flush out stains such as red fruit juice.

Bleach. Using bleach is like hiring the hit man after all peaceful persuasive methods have failed. When you've done everything you know how to do and there's still a stain, you may want to resort to bleaching. This isn't a step to be taken lightly, because bleaching can damage whatever you're working on, as well as alter the color. If it gets down to bleaching it or trashing it, it's an easy choice, but be sure to exhaust all the alternatives. See p. 33 for a breakdown of the various bleaches available and what they can be used on and safety precautions.

It's always a good idea to test any bleach on a hidden area, especially if you're not sure what kind of fabric you're working with. Whenever possible, bleach the whole object, not just the stained area—if something loses a little bit of color all over, it'll be a lot less noticeable than a single too-light spot. (When you're spot-bleaching, things can look pretty good until the object dries.) Be especially wary of spot-bleaching dry cleanables. Wetting the fabric before you apply bleach will make it work better. Always rinse bleach out as soon as you reach the color you want, and rinse well in between if changing types of bleach. Be sure to follow label directions to protect you and your possessions, and never use any stronger a bleach than necessary to do the job.

Apply a poultice. A poultice (a paste made by mixing a powdered cleaning chemical with water or solvent) will pull certain types of stains right out of porous materials. A paste made of a bleaching cleanser such as Comet plus water or lemon juice will often coax stains out of Formica countertops, for instance. Just cover the stain with the poultice and let it dry, then wipe away the powder after it dries. A poultice of absorbent clay (fuller's earth or kitty litter) and a solvent (paint thinner or dry spotter) will often suck oils stains out of concrete and stone. Poultices of other absorbents such as cornmeal or talc mixed with solvents can be used to draw oily stains out of wallpaper and unfinished wood and stone. Specialized stone-cleaning poultices are available for dealing with stains in marble, terrazzo, and other porous masonry finishes. K2r, the aerosol solvent spotter often so effective in removing oily or greasy stains from wallpaper, stone, and raw wood, is actually a poultice of solvents and absorbents.

Rinse. We rinse either between steps in stain removal, or as we finish up the whole process, to get all the spotting chemicals out. Most wet stain-removal procedures end with rinsing. I use "rinse" almost exclusively in this book to mean "rinse with water." For washables, this can mean holding a garment under the tap or dipping it repeatedly into a tub or basin of water. When we can't do this, as with dry cleanables, we have to resort to what's called "sponge-rinsing." This means sponging water through the spot using a clean cloth pad, keeping the wet area small and using an absorbent pad underneath to absorb the water. Always be sure to feather the edges as you finish. For carpet and upholstery, sponge-rinsing means sponging on clear water and then blotting it back out, taking care not to use any more water than necessary.

Rinsing isn't an optional step—if you skip the rinse you risk reactions between chemicals that weren't supposed to be there at the same time, and damage done by chemical residue left behind in your carpet or clothing. Unrinsed residues will also attract dirt like crazy to a freshly cleaned spot.

Air dry is what we don't usually do until the dryer goes on the blink and the laundromat is closed. It means turning it over to nature—natural air with maybe a sprinkle of sun and breeze but no motors or heaters, additives, or preservatives. Air drying is the safe way to get the water out, so we can take a closer look at our stainbusting results. When we've laundered or spotted something stained, we always want to air dry it so we won't set any stains that might still be lurking unnoticed.

Residue . . .
Will Never Do

Remember when Mother told you there was "iron" in the spinach and germs on your skinned knee? You looked good and hard and never saw either, you just accepted it on faith and ate the spinach and bore the iodine sting as it killed the germs. Time for some more faith in what I'm going to tell you.

When a stain or spot is gone—it seems to your very own eye that it's totally out, gone, not a trace left—there may still be something in there. Even though you can't see it, some of the cleaner, solvent, or soap that removed the stain may have remained in the fabric or on the surface. We professionals call this detergent residue, and if you don't get all it out, although it's invisible now it will: stiffen the spot, collect soil, and create its own stain—it can even deteriorate some fabrics.

This residue isn't hard to get out, and it's generally done with a rinsing agent. For alkaline spotters we sometimes use vinegar, a very mild acid. Most times, we just use a good thorough water rinse. This is one reason the final rinse step is so important, especially in carpeting. Don't get in a hurry and forget to do it.

Feather. We've all taken a spill out of something that's slightly dirty all over, only to end up with a highly noticeable "clean spot" that looks worse than the stain! Many spotters, including water, will also leave a ring when they dry, especially if the spot is allowed to dry in the center first, leaving a wet outer ring. To avoid things like this, we always want to "feather" or blend the edges as we finish up a stain-removal operation.

When you *apply* spotter to a stain, work from the outside in toward the center, to keep the stain from spreading. **Keep the wet area as small as possible.** Then, when you rinse, especially in the final rinse, work from the center back toward the outside, and blend the wet area into the dry area beyond with light, lifting, outward strokes. Instead of a distinct line between a wet spot and dry surrounding fabric, you want a graduated dampness, from wet to damp to almost dry.

You can also feather by blotting the dampened area as dry as possible between two clean dry cloths, then drying the spot quickly with brisk strokes from a clean towel. Or you can use a hair dryer, starting at the outside and working in toward the middle. The trick is to make sure the spot dries from the edges in toward the middle.

You never want to forget to feather as you finish up on dry cleanables and upholstery fabrics.

Catch It Quick,
Before It Can Stick . . .

(A Quick Recap of Stain Removal Strategies)

- Liquid spills. Blot up all you can and sponge the spot with water before it dries.

- Dry, powdery stains (toner, mud, etc.). Vacuum or dry-brush to remove all you can before applying any kind of liquid.

- Dry, crusty deposits. Scrape, then soak if needed to loosen stubborn stuck-on stuff.

- Oily or greasy stains. Use absorbent to suck up as much oil as possible before wetting the spot with solvent.

- Gum, tar, and other sticky stuff. Freeze, shatter, and scrape to remove the bulk of it before applying solvent.

- Penetrating stains (in stone, concrete, brick). Use a poultice to draw the stain matter out.

6

THE ROGUES' GALLERY OF STAINS

(From Easy
to Impossible)

Spots and spills happen to us every day, and a lot of them don't deserve a second thought. We drizzle a few drops of diet cola onto our slacks, or the dog jumps up and puts muddy prints on junior's jeans. Most minor incidents like these come out in the wash and are never heard from again. It's the minority, that little 10 percent of stains, that cause us 90 percent of our stain headaches. And most of these real bad guys crop up in the course of everyday activities like putting on makeup, polishing our shoes, painting the living room, cleaning the oven, or trying to improve the health of our houseplants. Here's a rundown on the whole range of stain villains, from the small-time hoods to the serious and repeat offenders, the especially dangerous and still at large.

Water-soluble stains. This gang contains the largest number of common stains, but they're the easiest to get rid of and generally give us the least trouble. Some of them are real pushovers. This group includes any staining substance (such as coffee, tea, soft drinks, fruit juice, water-soluble ink, wine) that can be dissolved and removed with water or water-based cleaners. Many of these stains come out with a simple laundering, if the stained item is washable. For the tough ones, and on dry-cleanable items, we use carefully chosen wet spotting agents to break down and remove the stain.

Greasy and oily stains. The second largest bunch, these are the stains containing grease, fat, or oil, and it usually takes a grease-dissolving solvent or water-soluble degreaser to completely remove them. Stains in this category include lubricating greases and oils, cooking oils, animal fat, and oily foods. Motor oil, Italian salad dressing, bacon grease, butter, and french fry spots are common examples. Some of these will come out of the washables with the aid of a laundry pre-treat. On dry-cleanable items, and for heavy grease stains on washables, we often have to employ a petroleum solvent to break down the oil. While many solvents will cut grease, the safest ones for you and your belongings are the nonflammable dry cleaning fluids described on p. 58-59.

Combination stains. These guys are tougher—they're the spots that have both greasy and nongreasy ingredients and require a multi-method attack to remove. Coffee with cream, gravy, creamy salad dressings, and chocolate are all examples of stains that contain oils, greases, and fats, along with starches, sugars, tannin, and other water-soluble stuff. A common mistake here is to remove the worst of it (the water-soluble part), and ignore the oily part. It may look all right until the oil darkens with age or heat to leave a permanent stain.

To avoid this, the rule of thumb for combination stains is to use the water-based chemistry first to remove the nongreasy ingredients, then apply solvents to get the grease and oil. The only exceptions are stains like lipstick, shoe polish, and mascara, which contain strong dyes in a wax base. You always start with dry solvent on these, because water can spread the dye and make the stain much worse.

Dye stains. Now we're getting down to the real bad guys. There are many stains in which the staining agent is a colorant or dye. Dyes are in everything from antibiotics to aftershaves to after-dinner drinks, sandals to suntan lotion to the Sunday papers. And some of them bond to fabrics so tightly they're impossible to remove. But many of them will come out if you just hang in there. The rule on dye stains is: Don't give up too soon. They're rough customers, but they can often be rehabilitated. If you have a tough dye stain like red Kool-Aid, red wine, or ink, stay with it—persistence often pays off.

Chemical stains. These are the hardened felons there isn't much hope for. When you're hit by one of these, look out! In chemical stains a chemical alters or destroys the dye in a fabric or surface—or the fabric or surface itself!—leaving a permanently bleached, discolored, or damaged spot. About all you can do is replace that section of the material (such as put a plug in carpeting), or put a doily or throw rug over the spot. It's hard to believe how many common household products contain chemicals that can injure or deface carpeting, upholstery, furniture, and clothes, and how little effort is made to make us aware of this fact. Since stains of this type are so deadly, let's take a close look at the most likely suspects.

- **Acne medications.** Surprise! Many zit killers (and some creams for fading age spots) contain benzoyl peroxide, a strong bleaching agent. It's hard to wash off your hands, so the stuff rubs off on chair arms and on the carpeting in front of the TV where teenagers lie, and usually doesn't start to bleach until it gets wet. High humidity or carpet cleaning can activate it days, weeks, or even months after it's deposited, and bleached-out orange or yellow spots begin to appear.

- **Acids and alkalis.** The strong acids found in many toilet bowl cleaners, tile cleaners, corn and callus removers, and even in vomit and urine can cause color changes in carpet and upholstery fabrics. Strong alkalis, such as the caustic lye (sodium hydroxide) found in many drain openers and oven cleaners, will not only devastate the dye, but often the fabric itself.

- **Bleaches.** We all know that liquid chlorine bleach will leave a lightened or bleached spot if we spill it on the carpet or spatter it on our clothes. But most folks don't realize that tracked-in pool chemicals, mildew removers, and even the milder laundry bleaches can also cause dye changes in textiles if left on for a long enough time.

- **Other chemical bad guys.** Some liquid plant foods and fertilizers will bleach out carpet dye, in case you ever wondered what those dull yellow spots were under pots and planters. Some pesticides can also discolor carpet if you're not careful when spraying baseboards. The suspect chemicals are malathion, diazinon, and DDVP. And the phenols in phenolic disinfectants have been known to fade carpeting as well as human skin, so there's more than one good reason to choose a safer, quaternary disinfectant for home use. (A "quat" is any disinfectant that lists some form of ammonium chloride as the active ingredient on the label.)

That's the stain gang, from least to worst!

7 STAIN SAFETY

(Playing It Safe for You and the Surface)

When removing stains we often use things that can burn, splash, dissolve things or create fumes, so there is a lot to watch out for, to make sure we live to enjoy our brilliant removal job. A dry cleaner in Alaska, for example, refused to clean my sleeping bag right before a big Scout trip. He explained that the toxic fumes from the dry cleaning solvent remain in the bag for a while afterward, and if you tuck your head inside to escape the mosquitos, it could be your last campout! An upholstery cleaner in California told me about a chair that was cleaned using flammable solvent spotters. The fabric seemed dry, so the man of the house sat down and lit up a cigarette—and the whole thing went up in smoke. Cats, too, have curled their little whiskered faces into solvent shampooed couches or recliners and been put to sleep permanently by the lingering vapors. Many of the chemicals used in stain removal can be hazardous if not handled properly. Don't panic and think a stain might be better than losing life or limb. But do follow these stain safety guidelines to keep yourself and others and your possessions and furnishings out of trouble.

First . . . Protect Yourself!

- Work only in a well-ventilated area—many spotting chemicals give off hazardous fumes. Expectant mothers should be especially careful. Well-ventilated means somewhere with fresh air flowing in and "bad" air flowing out—a room with windows open at both ends, or an exhaust fan going. Or outside on the deck, etc.

- Never smoke or work around flame or sparks when using flammable solvents (alcohol, amyl acetate, acetone, naphtha, some dry spotters). And you don't just get sparks from rubbing sticks together—sparks are created by light switches, the automatic starters in furnaces and many kinds of heaters, and even static electricity. So don't think this caution doesn't really apply to you.

- Put oil or solvent-soaked rags in a metal can when you're finished with them—they can catch fire spontaneously. (Yes, that means without any help from anybody.) And don't dry rags you used for solvent in a dryer.

- Don't even **think** of mixing two or three chemicals together so you can do several of the stain-removal steps in one fell swoop. Mix spotting chemicals only according to directions— some chemicals can create toxic gases when combined (and mixed chemicals will kill you a lot faster than mixed drinks).

- Store all hazardous chemicals up high or locked away out of reach of children—and make sure they have tight lids and clear labels.

- Strong acids, caustics, and solvents call for rubber gloves, not bare hands! It's smart, not sissy.

- Don't switch containers! It doesn't take long to forget what's in what, and some chemicals react with certain container materials. And even if we do write the new contents on the can, we always seem to go by the color and shape of the container, especially when we're in a hurry.

Second . . . Protect
What You're Working On

- Identify the stain **and** the fabric before applying any chemical— using the wrong stuff can set the stain or cause irreparable color loss and fabric damage.

- Take the time to think, look carefully, and read the label again.

- Work in good light, so you can see the stains and spots and the action.

- Stay cool—heat from hot-water washing, drying, or ironing can set many stains.

- Be patient—a little waiting (for the chemical to work) often accomplishes more than a lot of scraping and scrubbing.

- Be gentle—rubbing, squeezing, and beating with rocks only forces stains farther in and can do in the more delicate fabrics. Heavy-handed spotting techniques can distort, bruise, and fray fibers, leaving an ugly spot even if the stain comes out.

- Finish! Always flush or rinse out the spotting chemical when you're finished with a spot, and don't skip the in-between steps the instructions call for. Flush out one stain remover before applying another. This eliminates bad reactions between things. Letting chemicals mix together or dry out in the fabric can be damaging.

- Follow those label directions for mixing, storing, and using spotting chemicals. Used too strong or in the wrong order, some of them can weaken, fade, or even eat a hole in the very thing you're trying to salvage.

8

WORKING WITH YOUR DRY CLEANER

(When to Go to the Pros)

Deep down I'm a do-it-yourselfer. Doing it yourself is unbeatable . . . **if** you **can** do it yourself!

But we've all spent an hour and $5 worth of chemicals on a stain (and still not really gotten it out) when we could have taken it to a pro for $3.50!

I'm not talking about laundromat-level dry cleaning, either. Signs that say, "Do your own dry cleaning for 75¢ a pound" only tell you that you're on your own with what comes out—and bad spots and stains generally don't. If the solvent bath doesn't dissolve the stain, it'll still be there, only more visible, when that ballgown or bedspread emerges!

It may cost a little more, but don't think that what a dry cleaner makes is all profit. Whether you or they do the job, it still involves quite a bit of time to work on the stain, and often quite a bit of material. For ten or twelve dollars a few times a year, I'd take all the really troublesome things to the cleaners.

They're professionals! They want things to turn out perfect. So choose a favorite and stick with them. The more you work with them the more they'll work with and for you.

Professional cleaners have chemicals most of us don't have access to. They're highly effective, but also highly dangerous, and take expert training to use. The pros also have special tools like steam guns and a lot more of that irreplaceable experience than you or I. They face problem stains every day and on every imaginable surface.

They're your friends, but they're not magicians or faith healers. They can't restore lost color or serious damage or grow new hair on worn velvet or frazzled fur stoles. They're also not mind readers. They don't automatically know what's on something or what you did to the stain before you brought it in to them. Don't ever cut off tags or labels (even if **you** have them memorized), and that includes any labels on drapes, bedding, upholstery, hats, etc.

What else would dry cleaners say about how you can help them do a dazzling job?

- Let me do it all! Don't wash or dry or iron in stains before you bring them in.

- Let me do your wools, crepes, silks, taffeta or any questionable piece or fabric—I'll save you time and money.

- Don't wait! If it needs professional help, now is better and cheaper than later.

- Removing stains involves enough detective work already, so let me know or attach a note to the item explaining where and what you think the stain may be and how long it's been there.

- If the piece has a special problem—if something is injured or damaged—tell me please, so we won't end up blaming each other!

- Empty the pockets (**all** of them!).

- If you've tried some home remedy (or **any** stain-removal steps) already, be sure and tell me exactly what you did; maybe I can salvage the situation.

- Bring it in unravaged. Don't just say "Oh well, it's going to the cleaner anyway" and then toss it on the floor, drag it around, wad it up, or stuff it into a greasy car trunk. More damage is often done on the way to the cleaner than it had originally.

- Don't get your hopes up too high on anything decorated. Suede, fur or vinyl trim, velvet collars, anything with metallic threads, sequins, beadwork, appliqués, iron-on transfers, tassels, or fringes are between hard and impossible to clean, never mind remove stains from.

- Give me some breathing room—listen when I tell you, and accept the fact that I'll do the best I can, but there may be nothing anyone can do for it.

- In case you've wondered why we say we have to clean the whole thing, not just try to remove the ten-year-old toffee from it: It's because *we* want to be sure all spotting chemicals are completely removed when we're done, too.

KNOWING WHEN TO QUIT

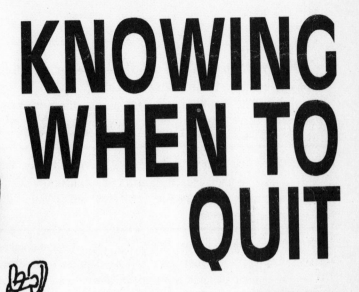

(The Truth About Certain Types of Stains)

Many of my TV and radio interviewers are call-ins, and what subject do you think always steals the show? You guessed it— stains. The trouble is that for an alarming number of the questions I can't give a useful or truly restorative reply.

---

1. "Mr. Aslett, my tub has black stains in the bottom, and I've used bleach, powdered cleansers, acid, lye and even sandpaper on it." "How old is your tub?" "Forty-six years."

---

2. "Mr. Aslett, I have this filthy thirty-year-old carpet full of stains from the dog I used to have. If I have it cleaned cleaned professionally what can I expect?"

---

3. (Believe it or not, I get asked this one a lot, too.) "Mr. Aslett, my husband smokes in the chair and we have cigarette burns on it and the carpet below— how can I clean them out?"

---

4. "Don, my kid scribbled on my latex living room walls with a permanent marker—what do I need to get it off?"

---

5. "Mr. Aslett, my boss has a favorite leather jacket he wears on the ranch. It's stiff and stained from twenty-five years of fence mending, and it has two bullet holes in it—how do I clean it?"

These questions, encouraged by the host who claims I know everything about cleaning, come five in a row and there's only one answer (and it's all bad news)—the coat is headed for the last roundup, the ink has penetrated not only the paint but the Sheetrock, and is now a permanent part of the decor. About all you can expect, ma'am, is a reasonably clean, worn-out carpet full of old pet stains. That carpet was dead ten years ago, and even if you could remove aged, set urine stains it wouldn't grow the pile back! And, sir, that tub is too far gone, trash it. The "stain" in the bottom is the cast iron showing through, you've worn off—scrubbed and bleached off—the porcelain!

Maybe with our favorite thing stained those aren't the answers we want to hear, but soils will be soils and some of them on the wrong thing at the right time and place produce a combination that spells termination for our treasures. Sometimes, in spite of your most dedicated efforts (and your A+ in high school chemistry), you run up against a stain you just can't lick. To save yourself from stain-removal stress, you'll know it's time to throw in the towel rather than use it when:

- You have to take the drapes down carefully so they won't disintegrate before you get them to the cleaners.

- It'll cost $12 to clean the strawberry pop stain off that $4.95 straw hat.

- The stain is still there after four trips through the washer.

- You're wondering how this stain will go with the six others on there.

- You've bleached the pants so many times they no longer match the jacket.

- The stain is right where you need to grip to try and get the zipper closed.

- The stain is the best-looking part of it!

- That's not a stain, it's *damage*. This includes:

   Anything badly scorched. Light scorch from ironing can often be removed, but heavy scorch is actual fiber damage, and won't come out.

   Anything burned—which means melted fibers and charred surface even if there isn't an actual hole.

Anything badly frayed. Shirt collars and cuffs abraded by whiskers and bracelets for example, will look dirty or stained even when they're clean, because the frizzed fabric reflects light differently.

Anything you've scrubbed or scoured to death. Once you've scored the smooth surface of your satin shirt, lacerated the lace tablecloth, or rubbed a bald spot in a velour armrest trying to remove a stain, it's never going to look the same—face it.

Part of the surface or material is gone—removed, destroyed, sanded, eaten away. (Moth holes and battery acid burns, for example, will still be there after all your efforts.) If you have a dropped-frying-pan burn in front of the kitchen stove, get a carpet layer to plug in a new piece and quit beating on yourself because you can't get it out with lemon juice and baking soda.

• The stain is purely and simply *permanent*.

Some stains just don't come out. Indelible inks, permanent markers, red food dyes, some medicines, and other dye-type stains sometimes just become a part of the fabric. To get them out, you'd have to strip **all** the dye out and then you'd be left with a light spot. Dye changes can be irreversible, too. Many common household products can alter or bleach dyes, leaving a permanent faded spot (see p. 88). The alcohol in cologne, perfume, and liquor can cause dyes to bleed and run in some fabrics, making a stain that can't be repaired. Even water will cause dye to run in some silks. And easily removed stains such as coffee, sugar, or blood can be set by heat, alkali, or acids to the point they become permanent. Sometimes a professional spotter can remove stains you can't get, but even the pros run across stains that just won't cooperate. They just mark them "permanent" and forget about them. That's what you should do, too.

• Sometimes it just isn't worth it.

If the fingernail polish puddle is in the middle of the living room carpet, you'll probably want to do whatever you have to get it out. But if it's on a twenty-dollar white acetate blouse, you'll spend more than that in time, chemicals, and energy trying to remove it, and the blouse will probably never be the same anyway. Might as well chalk it up to experience and buy a new one. Instead of spending half of Saturday trying to get the shoe polish off the cuff of an ancient pair of white chinos, why not demote them to painting pants and go play a game of golf? Some stains, even if ultimately removable, just don't deserve the effort and expense of getting them out.

I know it takes a lot of guts to retire a fifty-dollar Pendleton to a leaf-raking shirt and a lot of money to reupholster something or change a countertop. I've seen some of you diehards spend hours re-dyeing a dingy old towel Rit lavender, or trying to pick all the paint specks off a worn and faded slipcover. More power to your persistence, especially if stain removal is your hobby. Just remember that because it's your best or your favorite or unspeakably sentimental doesn't make it immune to permanent damage. We all have to go sometime and it's not wise to waste too much time trying to pull off a miracle— the smart spotter knows when to say when.

Stain-Salvaging Strategies, or "Creative Concealment"

When we come up against those stains we just can't lick, there's still one alternative left. It's called "creative concealment" —whimsical (and even some practical) things you can do with an impossible stain in an untrashable object. After all, stain injury is mostly cosmetic—the object in question is usually still perfectly functional.

- Amputate it—cut off the sleeves or legs, shorten the skirt, or carve, sand, or whittle it away.

- Embroider over it.

- Add a new button or pocket there, or a fabric flower or a decorative edging.

- Decorate it (reverse psychology approach)—add beads or sequins or a couple of complementary colors to it, outline it in black or silver.

- Cut it out and hem the edges (otherwise known as potluck peek-a-boo).

- Dye the whole thing darker, or that color, or dip the whole thing in the stain.

- Bleach the whole thing, or parts of it (tie-dye returns!).

- Repeat the stain at regular intervals.

- Turn it inside out, upside down, or around—or wear it backward.

- Restyle/remodel it. Convert it to a one-piece or a two-piece (you probably never liked the vest anyway).

- Depending on where it is on your clothing or curtain, you could add a belt or a tieback.

- Wear a corsage, campaign button, or big necklace over it, or a wide tie, scarf or shawl.

- Hold your arm, briefcase, or shoulder bag over it, or comb your hair over it.

- Set a rug, hassock, or potted plant over it or hang a picture or poster over it.

- Have a new piece patched in or have it rewoven.

- Disguise it by blending in the edges (with wax crayon or permanent markers, for instance).

- Paint, carpet, or texture the whole thing (after sealing the stain, in the case of painting).

- Hide the whole thing (if it belongs to somebody else).

- Send it to Seventh Avenue as a sample.

- Use it to fill a crack somewhere.

- Save it to make a scarecrow.

- Give it to Goodwill.

- Bury it with the body.

- Wear it to a Tacky Party.

- Cut it up for a quilt.

- Reduce it to paint rags.

- Recycle it.

- The "add an alligator approach"—sew an attractive appliqué or monogram or a pretty patch over it.

- Snip off a little piece of it to save for sentiment and get *rid* of the rest!

10

PREVENT THOSE STAINS!

(It's a Lot Easier Than Removing Them)

Have you ever met one of those people who can get more done alone than five of the rest of us put together? They don't seem to move any faster, work any harder, have any mysterious machine, they just get plenty-plus accomplished every single day at work and at home. Do you want to know their secret? It will not only solve 80 percent of your spot and stain stumpers, but a lot of your other life problems as well. My father was one of those miracle producers, and one day I finally realized how he did it.

Dad made a new livestock trailer, a beautiful blue rig we pulled behind the truck. When we returned from our first trip with it every side of the trailer was splattered, plastered, coated with mud, road tar, even gravel flung up by the tires. It took me two hours to clean it off and the trailer never looked quite as snazzy afterward. "I knew I should have taken the time to put mud flaps on it!" Dad announced. "Mud flaps?" I said. Dad quickly cut two pieces of rubber and tucked one in behind each tire. It only took a few minutes, and forever after, all we ever had was a bit of easily removed road dust on the trailer. That single thing saved hours of cleanup in a lifetime! My Dad did the same with everything on the ranch. He installed splash guards, bumper guards, oil finishes, haystack covers, and even a system in animal pens to prevent manure spots, chewing, rubbing, and pawing. Dad's secret in life management was that he didn't spend all his time repairing, restoring, cleaning up after—or de-spotting—he *prevented* the problem. That's not only a smart and cheap way to live, it's a lot easier on us and our surroundings and possessions.

Getting a stain out isn't as much of an accomplishment as we might think, because when we're finished (even if we've done a good job) we're still right back where we started. We haven't gained any ground. So why are we so often taught to solve problems instead of preventing them? Ninety percent of the ads

we see are for cures rather than preventatives. We can't wrap ourselves and everything we own in plastic, but we sure can take advantage of some antistain strategies. Bibs are a beautiful example. Wise women use them, but new fathers seldom seem to understand that one minute bibbing baby saves who knows how long swabbing, finding clean clothes, changing, and coddling later—not to mention laundry time.

People are amazed that my company cleans a commercial building in six hours after the previous contractor has been taking twice as long each night to do it. It's not magic, just prevention. We install good doormats, more and better trash cans and receptacles, educate the tenants, control building use and traffic, banish spotmakers, and guess what? It all eliminates work and damage. If we all found ways to prevent spots and stains at home, we'd not only be able to do without this and at least two dozen other books and pamphlets on stain removal, but thousands of gallons of cleaning chemicals, millions of hours of effort, and billions of dollars of costs. Successfully removing every spot may be wishful thinking, but preventing isn't.

The young mother who spreads a specially made tarp under her baby's high chair knows two important principles of prevention:

1. Messes are going to happen—they're part of living.
2. Spreading the tarp only takes fifteen seconds, but it'll take fifteen minutes to remove strained beets from the carpet—if we can do it.

We'll never totally eliminate spots and spills, but we can do a lot to keep them from becoming stains. It's better to know how to keep it out than how to get it out after it happens. Here are some excellent ways to do that.

The World's Greatest Stain and Spot Decoy—the Mat

So small, so unobtrusive, so inexpensive. Just lying there quietly, the right kind of doormat will stop thousands of spots and stains at the door, before they ever get in or on. It only takes one piece of cleaning equipment to clean a mat, and ten or more pieces to clean tar, mud, and animal mess out of the house once they get in. The American Carpet Institute claims 80 percent of the dirt in a home comes through the front door. Decoy it!

The best mats on the market for this purpose are olefin or nylon carpeting with a nonslip rubber back for inside, and crisp grasslike polypropylene mats for outside, to knock off the "big stuff" and withstand the weather for years. Just make sure they're at least four steps long, both inside and out. If you can't find a convenient local janitorial-supply store to buy them at, write to me at the Cleaning Center, Box 39, Pocatello, Idaho 83204, and I'll send you free information.

The Dynamics of a Drop Cloth

I'm a good painter, and can usually brush and roll without slopping any extra paint around. But I always put a drop cloth down, even for a ten-minute touch-up job. It takes a lot less time to throw a cover over the couch than it does to remove even a single paint spot from it. The ratio of time spent to clean up, compared to cover up, is about fifty to one! It takes no more than three minutes to carefully spread a drop cloth over something you want to protect. Cleaning it off later is at least a two-hour job—**if** you can get it off, and if you can live with the bleached, scuffed, deglossed surface you end up with after the cleaning process.

A good drop cloth (buy a heavy-duty canvas one about nine foot by twelve feet) costs around twenty-five dollars and folds up like a sheet in the garage closet or truck.

Don't ever use old newspapers; those things just strain the stains and hide them until they settle in good. They stick to your feet, and paints and liquids seep right through them. Another counterfeit drop cloth is the thin plastic type; what a loser. It sticks and clings to everything, and since it's transparent, holes and punctures are hard to see. So while you're enjoying the illusion all is well, the stain that sneaked through is firmly settling in for a long stay.

Dress for the Mess

You say you can't seem to win the stain war, because your job or situation is simply eight straight hours of stain exposure like painting, pottery making, mud wrestling, gardening, working in fast food or on cars? No matter how careful you are, you just can't win? Then you need to be especially sure to dress yourself and your surroundings for the sport. Don't pick cherries in white tights!

I always carry a set of coveralls in my car, for instance, since you never know when you may break down or need to carry something, get on or under something, use grease, or change a tire—and every one of these processes has amazing stain potential. If they get on your coveralls that's okay—they're a badge of honor, even—but nice they aren't on the new Shetland sweater! If you or your work are stain-prone, dress and design for it. Don't just say, "I won't get any on me this time."

The Napkin and the Hanky—Two Forgotten "Bulletproof Vests" of Stain Control

These two handy little helpers can take the rap for many a stain, and be a big assist both before and after. Don't leave home without them!

- On your lap: they can catch it before it lands.

- You can use 'em like a bib: to take the brunt of it, and a two-cent napkin sure beats a twenty-dollar tie.

- They can blot and absorb spills.

- They can be wrapped: around that sausage sandwich or ice cream cone, so food fallout falls on them instead of you.

- Can serve as a washer/dryer combination: wet one end and dry with the other.

- They make great hazardous-waste containers: to encase cores, peelings, not-quite-bare chicken bones, gum, and other gorys so they don't get a chance to stain.

- They can even be a dam: to keep spills from flowing further.

Invisible Shields

In addition to obvious protectors like napkins, drop cloths, and slipcovers, we can give many household surfaces and furnishings an invisible protective shield against staining.

• **Soil retardants.** Products like Scotchgard and Carpet Soil Protector seal the pores of fabric and give the fibers a clear protective coating. Like a coat of varnish, it's unstainable and keeps stains and even moisture out. Stains don't penetrate, so they can just be wiped right off the surface. Soil retardants not only keep liquid spills from sinking in but make dry soil a lot easier to vacuum or brush out. The fabric releases all kinds of dirt much easier because the soil is on the coating, not the fiber itself. Soil retardants are available for everything from carpeting and upholstery to suits and ties. Many fabrics and carpets today are treated with retardant right at the factory. Even when it's an option it's well worth the extra charge.

That doesn't mean it's stainproof forever, though. Time and use will wear off retardant and it'll need to be reapplied. And for maximum protection, it should be renewed every time you deep-clean treated carpet, clothing, or upholstery.

• **Masonry sealers.** Masonry is a magnificent and maintenance-freeing material—but not if it's left bare and untreated. You shouldn't have any exposed concrete, brick, stone, or earth tile that isn't protected by a clear masonry seal—and that even includes the grout. It only takes one experience removing smoke stains from an unsealed stone fireplace, or oil stains from a garage floor, to appreciate what sealers do. I sealed my fireplace twenty-five years ago and it still looks like new. You can get sealers that go on like varnish, leaving a smooth, glossy film, or the penetrating kind that hardly alter the original appearance of the material. Sealers are available at the do-it-yourself store or anywhere that sells masonry or tile. I like satin-finish sealer for vertical surfaces and high gloss for floors. Outdoors, be sure to use the kind designed for exterior use.

• **Wood finishes.** Raw or oiled finishes on wood floors, paneling, and furniture may look rich, but they're a mighty poor way of protecting that all-too-absorbent wood from stains, marks, rings, and smudges. You can get almost the same look with a coat of satin-finish polyurethane, and it'll keep stains out completely. A urethane finish requires almost zero care and it really speeds everyday dusting and cleaning.

• **Floor finishes.** Almost all sheet vinyl and tile floors will benefit from a layer of floor finish to protect them and help them resist staining. Black marks, for example, are a cinch to remove from a coat of wax. Even no-wax floors can be made prettier—and kept from eventually growing dull—with a coat of floor finish. My favorite is Top Gloss, one of the professional-quality, self-polishing, extra long-lasting waxes you can find at a janitorial-supply store.

Choose the Right Material

We set ourselves up for a lot of stains by the "characters" we surround ourselves with. Here are some of the most important ones to watch out for:

• **Carpeting.** The new stain-resistant carpet fibers are so much better at repelling stains than the older-generation yarns, it's silly to choose anything else—but some people still do. Some folks put carpeting in kitchens and bathrooms, too, but you're too smart for that.

• **Paint.** Even the best brands of latex flat paint (no matter what the label says) aren't very scrubbable. They're more porous, harder to clean, and much more prone to staining than semigloss latex enamel. If a matte look means that much to you, compromise and put on an enamel with satin or eggshell luster, which will stay spotless a lot longer.

• **Vinyl flooring.** To outsmart stains, you want no-wax—the clear top layer of no-wax flooring is much more stain-resistant than ordinary vinyl. And make sure it's sheet vinyl, not vinyl tile or anything with seams stains can seep down into.

• **Earth tile.** For floors, forget about raw, unfinished quarry tile, marble, slate, etc., or you'll forever be applying fresh sealer as foot traffic grinds and wears it away. You can get the same subtle look underfoot with satin glazed ceramic tile—and it's impervious to just about any stain. The protective finish is part of the tile, so it won't wear off. To head off stain headaches in the joints, get colored grout with a latex admix and be sure to seal the grout with a silicone masonry sealer.

• **Clothing.** Buy quality—stains come out of better-made brands and fabrics more readily than the bargain store specials. The more expensive garments often have built-in stain blockers—and even if they don't they'll usually repel stains better than bargain brands.

• **Bathroom fixtures.** Vitreous china fixtures (even the white ones!) are the best stain fighters, with porcelain-coated cast iron coming in a close second. Porcelain-coated steel is next best, followed by Corian and cultured marble. Fiberglass is the worst. Shiny chrome is the best brightwork, from a stain-resisting standpoint.

Eliminate the Source

The class bully informed me one day (when I was still a seventy-pound weakling) that unless I stopped flirting with the cutest girl in the class I was "cruising for a bruising." Likewise a lot of your possessions are aiming for a staining. Some of the major culprits you can eliminate without even missing them are:

• **Clothing.** Fitness centers were clever enough to ban the wearing of black-soled shoes, which mark up the racquetball courts, but we continue to scuff up our floors at home with them. And "mountain boot" soles not only black-mark floors, but constantly drip little gobs of mud and snow out of the cleats. And why have a leather jacket that constantly rubs dye onto your shirt collars, or a non-colorfast sweatsuit that bleeds color onto your undergarments? Just because they sell white silk toddler dresses doesn't mean you have to buy them. Don't build your life around hopelessly stain-prone things. If you live a white dinner jacket life, your closest and best friend will be the dry cleaner.

- **Red food dye.** Red is the worst color for causing stains. Cherry Kool-Aid is all but impossible to remove from non-stain-resistant carpet (and red Popsicles and red gelatin are almost as bad); lemon or lime comes out fine. Red-colored pet foods can make for impossible vomit stains, and Fido doesn't care whether or not his food looks "meaty" (he's color blind, after all). So why not fall for another color? White wine is more versatile than red and leaves you with less of a stain as well as less of a hangover. And white pasta sauces are less acidy as well as more fashionable.

- **Dye-altering chemicals.** Many common household products contain chemicals that can alter or destroy the dyes in clothes, carpet, and home furnishings, leaving a bleached or discolored spot. These include many toilet bowl cleaners, oven cleaners, plant foods, and insecticides (see p. 89). It only makes sense to seek safe substitutes for these products, or be extremely careful with them.

- **Toys.** Mean bright colors, loaded with potent dyes. Only you can decide if the benefits offset the risks in such things as colored modeling clay, crayons, Play-Doh, fingerpaints. Many of these products come in washable styles—it pays to check. At least you can hide the thirty-two-piece pen set and the poster paints when grandkids or guests' kids come.

- **Junk.** We all have odd bottles, boxes, cans, and tubes of aged and often totally unusable stuff lying around—everything from wood stain and spray paint to India ink and liquid shoe dye. I'm convinced we keep some of this stuff just for its stain and torture value! Things like this always get unleashed—dropped, crushed, broken open—at the worst possible time and place. And the stains from it hurt the worst because it wasn't even necessary. Getting rid of this junk is even better than putting it up out of reach of the kids and grandkids.

- **Markers.** Most of the things we use felt-tip markers for don't actually need permanent ink, but we buy permanent ones anyway. When we end up ruining a dress shirt or tablecloth, we always wish we'd gotten washable.

- **Medicines.** Iodine, mercurochrome, Merthiolate were good in their day, but we have antiseptics now that do the job without ruining carpets and vanity tops. Some cough syrups and cold medications have enough red or yellow dye in them to color Lake Michigan. Our sinuses aren't impressed with the pretty colors, but our blankets or bathrobes may be—why take a chance?

Watch Those Liquid Leavings!

Paul Harvey, the newscaster, does a nice scenario called "The Rest of the Story," wherein he shares with you the unseen, generally unknown part of a well-known event or personality. Now Don Aslett the janitor will do the same with a well-known commodity, "your liquid leavings." The half cup of pop or coffee you didn't finish, the one you left at home, at work, or while traveling; what became of it? Daily we all order and buy a drink of some kind, our goal being total consumption, total refreshment. Yet in reality when we've had enough we just leave the container somewhere with the remains, often right where we got tired of it—bus, car, or phone booth. Some of us tuck it under, between, or in back of something, some of us pour it on the ground, grass, or in the gutter. And some of us just pitch it in the trash.

When not dealt with intelligently, this liquid is a real problem. It gets tipped or kicked over, and not only causes stains and stickiness, but draws flies and other insects, and causes falls. Tossed in a waste container, it generally drips through a hole in the plastic bag, rusting or contaminating the waste container, and seeps out into the carpet. Once in the dumpster, it mixes with other liquids and develops into rancid brew fit for chemical warfare! When the dumpster is dumped and the contents compacted, the liquid drips out of the bottom of the truck all along the street.

We think our little bit of leftover liquid in the motel, school, or office is all there is. Think of three hundred or three thousand other people leaving their half cups of coffee, soft drinks, or water somewhere. That's a lot of buckets of loose liquid someone has to deal with. Who? a mother? the maid? the janitor? the garbageman? Once a container of liquid is in your possession, you own it, and if you're a decent dude, you'll take care of it either by chugging it or disposing of it properly. Leaving liquid to be spilled on people or things is pretty low class. If you can't finish it, take it to a sink or drain and dump it. You'll save someone the uncouthness of collecting it, and yourself and others a lot of stains.

Food Control

Twenty years ago, when my cleaning company was doing homes or commercial buildings, "spotting" (the official term for getting up spills and stains) was a minor assignment. But the amount of carpet we have today and the infiltration of fast food **everywhere** has swelled spotting into one of the primary pastimes of a cleaner. As high as 90 percent of the stains we get on carpets, clothing, furniture, and car seats are food spills. It only makes sense to try and **prevent** all we can.

Quitting eating is of course one alternative, but allow me to suggest a couple of other intake improvements that could lessen food fallout.

1. **Say where!** We professional cleaners see dramatic evidence daily that eating is what generates the most and the messiest cleaning. Whether or not eating is allowed there can make a drastic difference in the looks and life expectancy of a room or area and its furnishings. So declare certain places off limits! (How many activities are enhanced by eating simultaneously anyway?)

2. **Opt for a "stain-less" style of service.** How we serve has a lot to do with it, and buffet is about the worst. Offering food this way is coming right out and asking people to walk all over the house with it. Where there is carrying and moving around and balancing of plates on knees there will be dropping and spilling and smearing. Plus, in the case of a buffet, a lot of excess food lying around because everyone took a serving or two extra side dishes more than they could handle.

Far better to have all the eating done in one place at one time on the surface actually designed for it—a table. If you must serve elsewhere, make everyone sit down first and bring the food to them.

3. **The right container!** Paper plates and cups and like collapsibles are designed by the mission impossible people, they start to disintegrate the minute they're given to us. Even if you're a fast eater they last just long enough to give you time to fill them and assure a spill. Paper plates will always fold on you during second helpings because by then the cardboard is wet. There goes the carpet, your clothes, or the couch.

TIMING

(A reminder)

The sooner you get to it, the better the chances of getting it out.

The odds are against the procrastinators!

Fresh: 98%

Later: 44%

Next Month: 20%

				1	2	3
4	5	6	7	8	9	10
11	12	13	14	15	16	17
18	19	20	21	22	28	

A couple of party pointers

The average party generates thirty-one stains, twelve of which are on the best furniture and at least half of which are red dye base, plus four broken and seventeen left or lost things, three scratches, countless pounds of scattered litter and waste, and three long-distance calls on your bill.

The most obvious but seldom-practiced party precaution is to triple the waste containers throughout the party area, outside and in. Every guest (even the drunks) will look for a disposal site first, and if one is right at his elbow, he will make use of it, and others will follow suit. Likewise, once one slob slings sausage on the silk centerpiece, others will follow—you can count on it.

The second secret (secret because even though everyone knows it, no one does it) is that there is more to life and human affairs than trying to decide what and how much to eat. Limit the hors d'oeuvres and drinks to a non-messy select group. Two kinds of sandwiches and a couple of drink choices are plenty. More means indecision and waste in a guest's hand, and a mess later on yours.

At your next party put plenty of trash baskets around and pile up less goodies, and you'll have much less of a house hangover!

Car stains

Does your car get fifteen stains to the gallon? The more comfortable cars get, the more we live in them. Drivers' tests should really make us prove ourselves in **all** the real-life situations we find ourselves in—driving while drinking coffee or cola, while eating, feeding the baby, putting on makeup, writing, adjusting the radio, reading maps, quieting the kids, trying to wipe the windshield. My brother reconditions car interiors professionally and claims you can tell age, sex, religion, marital status, employment, hobbies, etc., from the mess and stains left behind in a vehicle. The tip-over odds triple in a car. Everything spills—if not right away, just give it a stop, turn, hill or lane change and it will. Almost any activity done while driving is about guaranteed to produce spots and stains.

The good news is that autos only have a couple of surfaces to stain. The bad news is, who carries any stain-removal equipment along with them? So spots set. The answer: I keep a small can of aerosol solvent spotter such as K2r for grease stains and a plastic spray bottle of all-purpose cleaner and several clean towels in my car trunk. Along with a pair of gloves and coveralls.

I keep a good supply of wet wipes in the jockey box, because clean hands do a lot to prevent spots and stains. And one of those hand whiskers or miniature carpet sweepers for crumbs. Cookie or chip crumbs, for example, have grease in them, and it'll sure come out when the sun heats things up. Plus a disposable dust cloth such as the Masslinn for general cleanup.

Then the first stop after they happen, or on a nice wide shoulder or turnaround if necessary, I get those spills and spots before they have a chance to become stains.

Camouflage

If you've ever had a white sofa and a black cat, you know why this is a good idea. Some colors and patterns don't just **show** every little mark and stain, they display and advertise it. Others can hide a host of ills and maybe even the whole cat. Here's a way to select clothes, flooring, wallpaper or furniture:

• **Color.** Earth colors in medium tones—not too light or too dark—are the best soil and stain hiders. White, yellow, and pastels show dark soil and any stain the worst.

• **Pattern.** This is the original way to make things hard to see—ask any anaconda. Small, dense patterns hide stains better than large patterns. Mottled, multi-hued fabrics like tweed hardly show anything, while a large expanse of solid color will show the slightest imperfection.

• **Texture.** A slight texture will aid the smudge-hiding ability of about any surface, from carpet to countertop to walls

and ceilings. An irregular surface reflects light in different directions, and makes spots and stains hard to see. Sculptured carpet, for example, is much more concealing than plush-cut pile. An orange-peel texture ceiling hides flyspecks and exploded champagne far better than stark, perfectly smooth paint.

MORAL OF THE STORY: If you live in Atlanta and your yard is red clay, choose a floor covering that hides rather than highlights the inevitable tracked-in dirt. If you're a young family just starting out it may be in your best interest to watch for a wall covering with flecks of pea green, strained-carrot orange, and handprint brown. You may not want to go that far, but it does make sense to take into account the kind of stains you're most likely to come up against and try to work around them.

It's nice to know that most prevention doesn't even involve any extra effort or expense, just a tiny bit of thought and planning.

Lame Brain
or Stain Brain?

We all do dumb things that get us in stain trouble. Here are a few of the bad habits it's well worth our while to break:

- Ignoring any spill (even water)

- Letting Baby Cakes run around "just a few minutes" with no diaper

- Tossing half-empty liquid anything into a wastebasket

- Leaving a wet paint lid anywhere

- Saving those miniature containers of hot sauce or Chinese mustard from the last take-out order

- Carrying an uncapped pen or marker in hand

- Touching anything but a napkin after you've eaten finger food
- Swaddling the bottle of Kahlúa you're hoping to sneak through customs in your best bathrobe
- Believing the baggage handlers can't possibly break the forty-eight-karat garlic dressing bundled securely inside your Samsonite
- Using your beloved Elvis beach blanket to cushion the gallon of cherry cider in the car trunk
- Eating take-out ribs in stop-and-go traffic
- Eating anything in a white suit
- Trying to sneak a sip of coffee while walking down the hall
- Thinking you can eat a pizza without six napkins
- Setting a cola on the dashboard "just long enough to fasten the seat belt"
- Leaving the boysenberry syrup boiling while you answer the phone
- Setting the open bottle of furniture polish on the stairs
- Ordering spaghetti while wearing a silk tie
- Leaving the roller tray of paint at the foot of the ladder
- Moving the ladder without taking the can of paint down first
- Slamming the front door with briefcase and mug in hand
- Leaving anything until later

Part II

WHAT'S IT ON?

(An Important Part of the Answer to "How Do I Get It Out?")

When we first start removing stains ourselves, some of them come out so easily we're amazed. Others elude our every effort, and it's hard to tell what we did wrong. The truth is that there are a lot of different materials out there, and they all react differently to stains and stain-removal techniques. When confronted with a stain, we immediately think: "What do I use to get it out?"—but the question we should ask first is: "What is the stain exactly (see p. 242-246) and **what is it on?**" A lot of ruined treasures tossed in dumpsters and landfills somewhere will testify to how many of us make rash moves and snap judgments here.

This section will help you handle correctly, identify, and prevent damage to all the common surfaces we find stains on. Since the majority of our stain problems occur on textiles, we'll concentrate a lot of our attention on these soft, porous materials. But we'll look at the hard surfaces that often pose a stain problem, too.

Soft Surfaces

The Facts of Life with Fabric

You just can't make sweeping statements, even about how to approach specific fabrics. Every textile begins as some kind of fiber—plant, animal, or man-made—but two fabrics made from the same fiber aren't necessarily treated the same. There are a great many types of silk, for example—and some are sturdy and easy to care for, others extremely delicate and almost impossible to clean. The way a fiber is spun, woven, dyed and finished makes a big difference in how durable, colorfast, and cleanable it is. Any lining, interfacing, or trim further complicates the issue. Just knowing you have a wool suit may not tell the whole story, because a little bit of vinyl or suede piping or a chalk stripe of acetate thread can drastically affect the way you'd treat it. To make things worse, the modern science that can make paper look like steel, gravel like granite, and plastic like pine has no problem making synthetics that perfectly imitate silk, and would-be wools that could fool a mother sheep. Which means most of us amateurs are instantly confused (when told not to use ammonia on silk, is it silk, rayon, nylon, or acetate, we wonder?). Ninety percent of us can't tell by the look or feel, so may I remind you of and direct you to one of your best buddies in stain removal—the label. A fabric care label is the safest way to tell how to treat a garment. By law, all clothing sold in the U.S. since 1972 must have a care label permanently attached.

Love Those Labels

The label must outline (in plain English) a safe cleaning method for the garment, and warn you if any standard cleaning procedures will do harm. Occasionally you run across one like I saw in an imported bathing suit that said "dry clean only," but most are clear and helpful. So leave those labels on, even if they tickle. Here's how to read between the lines of a label, in case you've wondered.

The label doesn't have to list more than one method if more than one can be safely used. If it says "hand wash only," you better assume that machine washing or dry cleaning would be bad news. You **might** be able to use one of those methods successfully, but you'd be doing so at your own risk—there's no guarantee. If it says "professionally dry clean only," assume

that machine washing, hand washing, or even coin-op dry cleaning could be harmful. If it says "machine wash, tumble dry," the garment is safe for machine washing and drying in all normal cycles and temperatures. If there are wash temperatures or cycles that would harm it, the label must state them. Likewise, unless it specifies what kind of bleach can be used (or says no bleach), you can assume that all bleaches are safe. If the label calls for ironing, but doesn't say at what setting, you can assume that even the highest heat setting can be used.

In addition, the Textile Fiber Products Identification Act of 1960 requires that all manufactured garments and household linens include the following information on product labels:

1. The natural or generic name of all fibers present in the amount of more than 5 percent of the total fiber weight

2. The manufacturer's name

3. If it is imported, the country of origin

So it's not like you're out there all alone—you at least have some federally mandated help in deciphering what you're dealing with.

If there's anything else you'd like to know about care labels, request the pamphlet "What's New About Care Labels" from: Federal Trade Commission, Bureau of Consumer Protection, 6th & Pennsylvania Avenue NW, Washington, D.C. 20580.

Labels on Furniture and Bedding

Manufacturers of upholstered furniture and bedding also have to attach a label showing the content of the filling (but not the cover material). Most furniture manufacturers do, however, include a label with approved cleaning methods. And you don't need a Sky King decoder ring to figure them out, either. Here's what those mysterious letters mean: W = Clean with water-base cleaner (shampoo); S = Use dry cleaning solvent only; WS = Safe for either wet or dry cleaning; X = Clean only by vacuuming or light brushing.

For carpeting, you may just have to keep track of what you bought, because there isn't usually anything anywhere on it to tell you what it is and how to care for it. The newest generation of nylons (the "stain-resist" carpets), especially, have some very specific cleaning instructions that have to be carefully followed or you'll void the warranty. So keep any cleaning information they give you when you buy carpet or furniture safely on file, so you'll know what to do when that inevitable emergency happens (or for that matter, what to do by way of regular cleaning).

What If There Ain't No Label?

Most of us have learned to recognize cotton and cotton/poly blends, and wool as well. (If your jacket smells like a wet dog when you come in out of the rain, it's probably wool.) But what do you do when there's no label and you don't have a clue? Use good old deductive reasoning, and proceed cautiously in the direction it leads you. Since 90 percent of the carpeting we use now is nylon, it is a pretty good guess that's what yours is. Most moderately priced upholstered furniture and virtually all auto upholstery can be wet-cleaned, so go ahead and try shampooing in an out-of-the-way place to see if it'll be okay.

Trying to figure out the fiber content of an unlabeled piece can be a tricky business, however. There are imitation silks out there that even a silkworm wouldn't suspect. But blends are the real bugaboo. Without extensive testing, it's very difficult to tell what fibers may be blended together in a particular fabric. Professional cleaners are trained to do it, and if you have a carpet or curtain or a piece of clothing you're not sure about, the safest approach is to turn it over to a pro. Certain fabrics, such as brocade, velvet, silk chiffon, taffeta, and watered silk are just plain hard (or impossible) to clean successfully without special training and equipment. If it's valuable, and especially if it's an antique, turn the job over to an expert dry cleaner—the peace of mind will be worth the price, and the piece will still be worth keeping afterward.

For spots and spills on everyday fabric with no labels, here are some rules that can help keep you out of trouble:

1. Pretest. I've said it before, but I don't want you to ever forget it! Use an inconspicuous part of the garment, carpet, or furniture to pretest the prospective spot remover (even water). Put on a drop of solution that's twice as strong as you intend to use, let it sit for longer than you would in the actual stain-removal process, then blot it out. If there's any color change or fabric damage, STOP right there—don't use it.

2. If it's delicate, go easy. Loose or extremely fine weaves, antique cloth, brocades, etc. can be damaged by rough handling. Tamp, scrape, or dry brush very gently (if at all) to avoid fraying, bruising, or dislocating fibers. Avoid the use of heat or harsh chemicals if gentler methods will do the job.

3. If it's shiny, be extra wary of using water. Some lustrous fabrics such as taffeta or fine silk will water spot like crazy, and should only be treated with dry spotters. Some moirés (fabrics with that wavy watery look) will be **ruined** by water. The safest approach for such tender morsels is to take them in for expert dry cleaning.

4. Get professional help if you need it—these people are your friends. A pro carpet cleaner can not only identify your carpet fiber, a good one can even tell you which generation of nylon it is! A dry cleaner you use regularly should be willing to help you distinguish between things you should bring in and ones you can handle simple spots on yourself. Even if you have to pay for the advice once, it's worth knowing which way to turn.

For a full explanation of the stain-removal techniques specified in this section, see Chapter 4. For descriptions of the spotting chemicals, see Chapter 5.

A Few Words About Individual Fabrics

As I said earlier, fiber is the starting point for all fabrics. There are two basic types—**natural**, which come from plants or animals, and **man-made**, which come from a laboratory.

Natural Fibers

Natural fibers from plants are called cellulose fibers, and this group includes cotton, linen, and ramie. Fibers created by animals are known as protein fibers and include silk and wool. The cellulose fibers tend to be absorbent, so they pick up stains easily, but they usually give them up without a serious fight. The protein fibers are fairly stain-resistant, but also fairly sensitive to chemicals, so we can't always use the most effective weapons in our stainbuster's arsenal on them.

Here are some general guidelines on different types of fabrics and how you can expect them to react:

Fiber; Found in	Stain characteristics	Cautions
Cotton Light- and medium-weight garments, linens, handkerchiefs, slipcovers, curtains; often blended with polyester in permanent-press garments	Very absorbent so it picks up stains easily, but it also responds well to removal measures; subject to mildew	Handles most spotters but is sensitive to acids—don't use vinegar on it; withstands heat well.
Linen Blouses, dresses, summer suits, household linens, and other articles	Absorbent so it stains easily, but not as bad as cotton	Shares cotton's sensitivity to acids and mildew; high heat okay
Ramie Light and medium-weight garments. Blended with cotton in sweaters	More stain-resistant than cotton or linen	Sensitive to acids, but fairly mildew-resistant; handles heat well
Silk Light and medium-weight garments, scarves, home furnishings	Fairly stain-resistant due to the smoothness of fiber. Susceptible to yellowing from alkalis, chlorine bleach, high ironing temperatures, perspiration, and exposure to sunlight. Stain removal often difficult because silk is sensitive to so many different chemicals.	Many silks water-spot, and require dry cleaning. Damaged by ammonia, vinegar, harsh alkaline cleaners, digestants and chlorine bleach
Wool *(including alpaca, angora, camel's hair, mohair, and vicuña)* Light-, medium- and heavy-weight garments, coats, blankets, carpeting	Naturally water-repellent so it resists many stains; but removal of stains from wool is difficult because of its sensitivity to chemicals	Damaged by ammonia, digestants, alcohol, harsh alkaline cleaners, chlorine bleach—most woolens require dry cleaning or gentle handwashing, cool air drying

Man-made Fibers

Though some man-made fibers were produced on an experimental basis as early as the mid-1800s, they've come into widespread use only in the past forty years. In that short time the list of man-made fibers has expanded to include twenty-one generic names and more than two hundred trade names, so it can get a little confusing. Because of their nonabsorbent nature, most man-made fibers are fairly resistant to water-based staining agents, but some of them actually attract oily and greasy stains. Synthetics also tend to hold onto stains tighter than natural fibers—they don't give 'em up without a fight. While synthetics are generally resistant to chemical damage, a few of them are ultra-sensitive to certain of our stain-fighting chemicals, and most don't tolerate stain-removal procedures involving heat well.

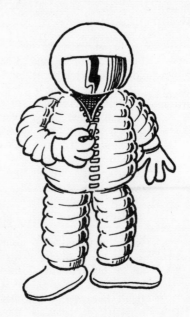

Fiber; Found in	Stain characteristics	Cautions
Acetate (*Airloft, Celanese, Avron, Estron, Lanese, Loftura, etc.*) Apparel, lingerie, linings, draperies, upholstery, fiber fill for quilts, pillows, and mattress pads	Good resistance to stains and mildew; susceptible to color fading and dye running	Damaged by acetone, vinegar, alcohol; sensitive to heat; most acetates must be dry-cleaned or washed as delicates
Acrylic (*Acrilan, Creslan, Fina, Orlon, Pa-Qel, etc.*) All kinds of clothing (especially sweaters), pile fabrics, blankets, robes, carpet, drapes	Good resistance to stains and mildew	Sensitive to heat—always use warm water, dryer, and iron settings
Modacrylic Deep pile coats, blankets, children's sleepwear, fake fur, stuffed toys	Good resistance to stains and mildew	Extremely heat-sensitive—no hot-air drying, always use lowest iron setting
Nylon (*Anso, Antron, Cantrece, Caprolan, Celanese, Cordura, Ultron, etc.*) Blouses dresses, hosiery, lingerie, jackets, bedspreads, curtains, sleeping bags, tents, carpet	Very good resistance to most stains, especially oily and greasy ones; white nylon will yellow in sunlight, and will pick up fugitive dyes if laundered with colored garments	Somewhat heat-sensitive—hot water okay but use warm dryer, iron settings
Polyester (*Avlin, Caprolan, Dacron, Fortrel, Hollofil, Kodel, Shanton, Trevira, etc.*) Blended extensively with cotton, rayon, and wool for use in all types of garments, especially permanent-press items; also fiber fill for pillows, jackets, etc.	Good resistance to non-oily stains, but attracts oily stains; resistant to sunlight, mildew, and perspiration	Moderately heat-sensitive—warm water, dryer, and iron settings are best choice

Fiber; Found in	Stain character- istics	Cautions
Rayon *(Avril, Durvil, Zantrel, etc.)* Blouses, dresses, lingerie, rainwear, slacks, sportswear	Good stain resistance; susceptible to mildew	Slightly susceptible to acids (use vinegar sparingly); resin-treated rayon may be damaged by chlorine bleach; use medium heat
Spandex *(Lycra)* Foundation garments, swimwear, athletic apparel, ski pants, support hose, elasticized fabrics	Good resistance to stains, body oils, perspiration	Damaged (de-elasticized!) by chlorine bleach; very heat-sensitive—use lowest dryer and iron settings
Triacetate *(Arnel)* Permanent-pleat garments, dresses, flannel, jersey, taffeta, textured knits, tricot, sportswear	Good stain resistance, but subject to mildew	Damaged by vinegar, acetone, alcohol; withstands high heat well

Three Troublesome Fabrics to Stay Alert For

Silk. Silk fabrics vary enormously in the care they require and how they respond to cleaning. Though most have to be dry cleaned, some silks can be washed successfully and others will bleed dye at the drop of a hat. As noted earlier, silk fiber is sensitive to acids, alkaline detergents, ammonia, enzyme digesters, and chlorine bleach (did you notice that this list includes almost all of our really potent stain removers?). Silk is also extra-delicate and easily abraded and very likely to water-spot. If you get a serious stain on a silk garment that's important to you, take it in for professional cleaning. If it's one you ordinarily wash, you can try the stain-removal methods recommended for that particular stain, but take it slow and easy.

Wool. Doesn't like rough handling or harsh chemicals either, and that includes heat, alkaline detergents, ammonia, alcohol, and chlorine bleach. And digestants will snack their way right through it. It's more tolerant of water—though a 100 percent wool garment will probably shrink when soaked with water, wool blended with synthetic fibers can often be washed on a delicate cycle, or hand washed. Many woolens and worsteds will also stand up to a little tamping and scraping. You need to be very careful about rubbing or scrubbing wool when wet, though, or it can "felt" and shrink. You should be able to remove many stains from wool yourself, but if it's a valuable piece, calling in a professional cleaner will be a lot cheaper than ruining it. Coffee has a real affinity for wool fiber, and it's particularly hard to remove from light-colored woolens.

Velvet. Soft, plushy surfaces can be deceiving. Many of the new synthetic (acrylic and nylon) velvet and velour upholstery fabrics wear like iron and clean up like stainless steel. And cotton velveteen is usually pretty durable, and can be laundered like any delicate fabric.

But the older velvets, many of them made of silk, wool, and other delicate fibers, are very easily damaged and require special care. Some velvets may never recover from being hung on the wrong kind of hanger, so you can bet they'll be ruined by careless cleaning. If you have an older garment with a velvet collar, an antique chair, or any velvet you're unsure of, take it in for professional cleaning.

With any plush fabric, take care not to crush the pile or create a bald spot with harsh scrubbing. And when you're finished spotting, brush the pile all one way, or it'll dry out with a splotchy look.

Other Sensitive Softies

Leather. Finished leather, the kind that's been dyed and has a smooth, lustrous finish, resists stains fairly well. You always want to go easy with water on leather. On finished leather, try wiping spots off with just a plain dry cloth—you'll find many soils will succumb to this simple treatment. Wipe any remaining soil away with a sponge or cloth dampened with lukewarm water and a mild soap such as saddle soap. Then buff dry with a clean cloth. You can't use dry spotters or solvents on leather because they dry it out, and no matter what the hint and tip columns say, don't put rubber cement on hidebound grease stains. When something leather gets a serious stain such as ink, dye, paint, glue or nail polish, hasten it in for professional cleaning. The cleaning process will also restore the oils to the skin to keep it from drying out and cracking, and should be done every year or two in any case.

Unfinished leathers such as suede, shearling, and split cowhide are another matter. These have no protective finish, so they slurp up stains fast and hold on to them forever. You really

can't do much about removing spots from this kind of leather yourself, beyond brushing it with a suede brush. Have your unfinished leather treated with a water repellent to minimize stain penetration, and take it in for professional cleaning as soon as it's needed. Don't wait until there's a lot of heavy, ingrained soil for the cleaner to deal with. But bear in mind that not all dry cleaners are equipped to deal with leathers and furs; look for a cleaner who specializes in leather.

With all leather garments, wearing a scarf to protect the collar from body oils and makeup will help head off stains and greatly extend the time between cleanings. (Now we know why all those WWI flyers wore scarves.)

Carpeting and Upholstery

Of all we own, we probably treat our carpets the worst. We tromp on them, push heavy furniture around on them, and drop, slop, spill, and drip everything from gravy to grape juice to axle grease on them. It's a testimony to the carpet industry that they stay looking as good as they do, in spite of us.

The big crimp in our style when it comes to destaining carpet and upholstery is that spotters can't be flushed through the fabric like they can in most garments. It's a real help to be able to flood water or spotting chemicals right through the fabric from the back side to the front, so the stain is pushed back out the way it came in. With clothes, too, we can use as much liquid as needed to "wash" stains entirely out of the fabric. But with carpets and upholstery (and some garments with padding, lining, etc.) we don't have that kind of freedom, so we have to alter our technique a little.

Because we're forced to work from the face of the fabric, we have to be careful not to drive stains deeper as we go. So we want to be extra sure to use absorbents and blotting action to remove as much of the stain as possible before applying any chemical. And here especially dry-brushing and scraping should be done in such a way as to lift soil and stain matter up and away from the fibers, rather than force it into the pile.

We also have to be careful not to over-wet the fabric, because getting the carpet pad, furniture filling material (or garment lining) saturated with either wet or dry cleaners can create a lot of headaches. Solvents attack many of the foam fillings and latex adhesives used in carpet and furniture construction, and colors can bleed out of wet backing and filling materials and stain the cover fabric. So we have to use as little liquid spotter as possible, and compensate by leaving it on the fabric longer and using gentle agitation to break down the stain. Since all the chemicals we use here have to be blotted back out—and rinsed, and the rinse water blotted out too—it just makes sense to go easy on the liquid. Stains that reappear in carpets and upholstery are largely a result of not enough blotting (see p. 146). When you pour on the juice and don't blot it all back out, it carries the stain down deep into the fabric, where it will just wick back up as the item dries. The spot may look okay when it's wet, but a hurry-up stain-removal job on carpeting or upholstery will usually come back to haunt you.

In general, you can use the procedures outlined for "Dry Cleanables" in Part III of this book—"How to Go About It"—on carpeting, upholstered furniture, and vehicle upholstery. Just remember to rinse and blot thoroughly, as outlined above, and you'll be down there taking out carpet spots like a pro.

Oriental Rugs (and Other Valuable Floor Coverings)

If you have a valuable oriental or a prized antique rug, don't be too quick to start spotting it yourself. There are so many possible combinations of dyes and fibers, some of them pretty sensitive to rough handling, that you can't generalize about the care of art underfoot. Take it to a professional cleaner who specializes in cleaning such pieces, and count it money well spent.

Carpet Spots That Reappear

We've all had freshly cleaned spots in carpet come back to haunt us. A few hours or even days after cleaning, they miraculously (and maddeningly) reappear. What this means is that we didn't completely remove them in the first place. We got the surface of the pile clean, but there was still stain matter or detergent residue buried deep in the carpet. As the pile dries, the water evaporates from the tips of the yarn first, which prompts more moisture to wick up from deep in the carpet. If any stain material remains, it migrates up to the yarn tips along with the moisture, and leaves the face of the carpet stained again when it's dry.

When it comes to oil and grease stains, if you don't get it all out the oil itself wicks back up to the surface as you walk on the carpet, and becomes highly visible again as it attracts and holds dirt.

To avoid reappearing carpet spots, clean and rinse anything beyond surface spots thoroughly, using enough liquid to get down to the roots of the pile without soaking clear through into the pad underneath. When you're finished, put a thick, clean, absorbent towel on the freshly cleaned spot and weigh it down with a heavy book or a brick. Leave it there until the carpet is thoroughly dry, and all the moisture and any remaining stain stuff will wick up into the towel.

Mattresses, Pillows, and Other Padded Surfaces

The cover fabric on most mattresses will stain from just about any kind of spill, and deep cleaning is difficult, so protection is the key. All mattresses should be covered with a mattress pad (and you might well want to put a waterproof mattress cover under that for young children or the bed-bound). Then you can soak, wash, apply digestant, etc., at will to any stains on the pad. The surface of the mattress itself will be protected. If the mattress cover does get a stain, it can be lightly shampooed or

spotted with dry cleaning fluid, but you don't want to get the padding underneath wet. To remove stains from mattresses, treat them just like upholstered furniture. Use the "Dry Cleanables" instructions in "How to Go About It;" be careful not to over-wet, and blot thoroughly to remove any spotting chemicals you use. Feather the edges to avoid leaving a water spot.

For pillows, protection with pillow cases will do a lot to prevent staining. Isolated spots on pillows can just be lightly sponged with the appropriate chemical, then rinsed, blotted, and feathered, as described for mattresses. The same is true of quilted items, stuffed toys, soft sculptures, etc.

Although many pillow manufacturers recommend dry cleaning, most pillows can be successfully machine washed and dried (use the delicate or gentle cycle, low heat). Feather pillows should be washed in a gentle soap such as Woolite and tumble dried without heat. Check the care label if there is one for instructions. Be forewarned that inexpensive synthetic fill pillows may go lumpy when washed.

Skin. Well, it is a soft surface, isn't it? And it does get stained. The best way to take care of stains on your hands is to avoid them. Wear rubber gloves for such stain-prone activities as polishing shoes or canning blueberries. Or if gloves cramp your style, rub one of the "liquid glove" products into your hands to seal out the mess before you change the oil in your car or paint the back porch. Liquid Joy works well for this purpose, too—just rub a small squirt of the stuff into your hands like hand lotion. When you're through with the messy task, all the grease or paint or whatever will wash right off. For taking off stains that do get on your skin, the waterless hand cleaners mechanics use work quite well. Just remember that skin is sensitive and it absorbs chemicals, so don't use strong stain-removing solutions and solvents on your hands or any skin. Better to wash with a mild soap, put on some hand lotion, and wait for the stuff to loosen by itself than to risk an allergic reaction or absorption of some dangerous chemical.

Paper. True, paper isn't really soft—but most papers aren't really hard either. For the most part paper is extremely porous, though, so it sucks up stains like a sponge. We've learned to take care of most paper stains with erasers, correction fluid, or retyping. And many nongreasy spots can be gently wiped away with a clean damp cloth, if it's a paper with rag content, such as watermarked bond. Even if you happen to slop coffee on your term paper just minutes before it's due, there's hope. Sponge the paper quickly with a mild vinegar solution, then press it with a warm iron. Use blotters or press cloth when doing this, to prevent scorching. It may not look quite as good as Natalie Neat's submission, but it'll be better than it was.

For inexpensive posters or prints (or any paper) with fingerprints or oil stains on them, first rub the spot with an art gum eraser, then sponge with lighter fluid or spray with K2r. Don't try these tactics on valuable art prints or first editions or watercolors though—take them to a professional art restorer. And make sure all art prints or objects are professionally glassed and framed or cased for protection.

Wallpaper. Most "wallpaper" isn't paper anymore. Most of it is either solid vinyl or vinyl-coated paper or cloth. So the surface you're working with isn't paper, it's vinyl. Even vinyl wall coverings vary in their cleanability, with the higher-priced ones usually being the most stain resistant and cleanable. Solid vinyl wallcoverings can withstand quite a bit of rubbing and scrubbing, while the cheaper thin-coated papers can be damaged by any heavy-handed stain-removal procedures.

The first step in removing wall covering stains is to try dry wiping, either with an art gum eraser or "dry sponge," available at a janitorial-supply store. Next try wiping gently with neutral detergent solution, but be careful not to wet the seams. For the sturdier papers, more aggressive stain-removal techniques can follow, using the chemicals recommended in Part III. Be sure to pretest all spotters in an out-of-the-way place first, though— some stain solvents make the dyes in wall coverings run, and the pattern can be scrubbed right off some of the cheaper papers. See "Vinyl Fabrics" for chemicals that shouldn't be used on this popular plastic.

If you still have wallpaper up from the days when it **was** just patterns dyed on porous ol' paper, you probably won't be able to use any water on it. Just wipe it down with a dry sponge.

Those Temperamental Ties!

The man's tie!!! I agree—what could be dumber than a piece of overpriced cloth tied around our neck to prove to the public that we are indeed dressed up. No wonder it gets so many stains—it's in the perfect place to drag through everything and catch drips, dandruff, food fallout, and grease from our hands when we go to straighten it. Cleaning your own ties (especially **silk**) is treading on treacherous ground. These little devils are cut on the bias, so the fabric distorts very easily, and most have a lining that's prone to wrinkle and shrink. Even professionals have a hard time cleaning a silk tie so it looks right afterward.

You don't want to mess much with madras, either— the dye in them runs all too easily. Wool is more workable— you can usually spot these yourself. Just follow the instructions in Part III for that particular stain, including all the cautions for wool. Then press the tie when you're through if it needs it, using a press cloth.

I remove minor grease spots from my ties with dry solvent spotter (here's an excellent place to use your feath-

Vinyl fabrics. Including furniture and vehicle upholstery, clothing, etc. The safest course is to just wipe it with neutral detergent solution—since vinyl is fairly nonabsorbent, most stains will come out with a little patience. Don't ever use dry cleaning fluid, lacquer thinner, acetone, or nail polish remover on vinyl. Any kind of volatile solvent can soften the plastic or leach out

ering skills). If I get a nongreasy stain on a tie, I do something I wouldn't do anywhere else. I wet a large area around the stain with dry spotter, then quickly put wet spotter (or even just soap and water) on the area of the stain only, right on top of the wet solvent. Then I blot the whole thing dry with a towel and feather the edges—this method helps to avoid water marks and it works amazingly well most of the time.

When one of my favorite ties gets a major stain, or gets to looking tacky overall, I give the dry cleaner a chance at it. If it's just a plain old everyday tie, I simply replace it.

To keep your ties looking as good as possible for as long as possible, it wouldn't hurt to cut down on tie-endangering habits and practices, such as letting the end drop down into your dish when you bend over to sit down at the table . . . taking them off and hanging them on doorknobs or chair backs or car fenders . . . tossing them in the back seat or into overstuffed drawers or onto cluttered dressers tops . . . stuffing them in suitcases carelessly (too close to the aftershave), or closing the suitcase on them. And don't be ashamed to tuck your tie inside your shirt when you sit down to soup or a juicy hamburger. (You could also switch to bolos or bow ties.)

the plasticizers, leaving the surface dry and brittle. Don't use gum freeze on it either, because vinyl can crack or shatter when ultra cold. And steel wool or any kind of abrasive or harsh scraping can remove the pattern from the surface, or score it. Applying petroleum jelly (leave on for up to 30 minutes) will often help lift stains off vinyl.

Hard Surfaces

Stains aren't as big a threat to most hard surfaces as they are to textiles. Many of the hard surfaces we deal with, such as window glass, chrome, porcelain, and glazed ceramic tile are so nonabsorbent as to be almost stainproof. Slightly more porous surfaces such as painted walls, vinyl floors, and plastic laminate (Formica) countertops are susceptible to some types of stains, but are by and large impervious to most spills. Removal from these relatively nonpermeable surfaces often involves no more than a quick swipe with a damp cloth. If you have highly porous hard surfaces such as raw wood, concrete, brick, or stone that aren't properly sealed against stain penetration, read Chapter 10 before you do another thing.

For stains on hard surfaces, you use the same solvents and cleaning chemicals you do on textiles; you just have to adapt your attack to the surface you're working on. For instance, hairspray will take ballpoint ink off cultured marble just as well as it will off a white shirt. But instead of flushing it through a fabric, you need to spray it on, let it sit a few seconds, scrub gently with a white nylon scrub pad to work it loose, then wipe it away.

The pretest rule applies to hard surfaces, too—remember to try any questionable cleaners in a hidden area first to make sure they won't do harm. Don't use strong solvents like acetone and lacquer thinner on paint, vinyl, varnished wood, or Plexiglas or other plastic (including plastic laminates such as Formica). Solvents can soften and damage these materials. You can safely use such volatile solvents to remove stubborn stains like paint, fingernail polish and glue from glass, chrome, china, porcelain, earth tile floors, and other chemically resistant surfaces. Following are some specific surfaces and tips for how to deal with them.

Raw wood. The only good advice I can give you regarding raw wood is: Don't have any! Some designers like to leave certain types of wood planking (especially redwood and cedar) raw and unfinished. While this can result in a nice natural look and outdoorsy aroma, it won't stay handsome long. Any kind of stain will sink right into the porous surface, and be very difficult to remove. A dye stain, such as ink or food dye, will be virtually impossible. The pores in wood were designed to transport liquid, and transport it they will—many stains will sink in so deep you can't even sand them away. And you can't use a lot of water on raw wood without swelling the grain.

Soft woods stain the worst of all, but all wood should be protected with a sealer or finish of some kind, the best probably being polyurethane. Polyurethane or varnish with a low-luster or flat finish will enable your wood to still look expensive while preventing stain penetration. Danish oil-type finishes are much better than raw wood, but nowhere near as good as urethane or varnish-like coating.

For stains on existing raw wood, try the spotting chemicals recommended for that specific stain in Part III, followed by light sanding if necessary. Then get that sealer on there!

NOTE: Much so-called "wood" paneling really isn't wood at all, except for the cheap plywood or pressboard base sheet underneath. The rich-looking grained surface you see on such panelling is actually a thin sheet of vinyl bonded to the panel, with a picture of real wood printed on it. The dead giveaway is that you can see the same grain patterns repeat from one sheet to the next. If your "wood" paneling is of this type, follow the instructions for vinyl under "Vinyl Fabric" and "Wallpaper."

Raw stone, brick, and concrete. Ditto what I said for wood. The only masonry surface I wouldn't put a sealer on would be something extremely hard and smooth like polished granite. Anything else, I'd seal. If you have existing stains on fine stonework such as polished marble, get one of the poultice stone cleaners sold by specialty cleaning outlets especially for this purpose. HMK Stone Care System, distributed by SNS, Inc., 425 Brannen Street, Suite 210, San Francisco, CA 94107 (415-546-3822), has a complete line of stone cleaners and sealers. For concrete, brick, and rough stonework, you can use the concrete cleaners and stain removers sold by janitorial-supply stores.

Once you get it cleaned up, put a coat or two of masonry seal on it to keep future stains from sinking in. If the masonry in question is outdoors, make sure it's an ultraviolet resistant sealer, designed for outdoor use.

To remove fresh oil stains from concrete, sprinkle them with kitty litter, grind the litter in with your foot, and let it sit until the oil is absorbed. A final wipe with paint thinner should take care of any remaining traces.

Vinyl floors. The newer, no-wax vinyl floors are more stain-resistant than their predecessors. The top layer of clear vinyl on these floors is so thick, hard, and glossy most stains won't penetrate it. Here, too, you have to avoid strong solvents like acetone and lacquer thinner, which will soften the plastic, but most household stains and chemicals will wipe off with no damage. If you have an older floor, it's probably sheet vinyl, vinyl composition tile, or maybe even vinyl asbestos tile. If it's really old, it may be linoleum. These materials aren't as impervious to stains and chemical damage as no-wax flooring, so you have to protect them. If you'll keep a good coat of floor finish (wax) on these floors, stains are very likely be confined to the wax. If you get a bad stain, all you have to do is scrub up the discolored floor finish and rewax—the flooring material underneath is still untouched.

Don't use steel wool, powdered cleansers, or anything abrasive on any type of vinyl flooring, except as a last resort. And watch what you're doing when you scrape.

One very troublesome stain on vinyl flooring is caused by color bleeding from a vinyl-backed floor mat or throw rug that is kept in one place for too long. The vinyl has plasticizers in it to keep it soft, and they will eventually migrate out of dark-colored mat backing into the vinyl of a light-colored floor, leaving an ugly stain. Such stains can often be lightened by scrubbing, bleaching, and exposure to sunlight, but often are impossible to remove entirely. The only real cure is prevention—don't leave mats or rugs with dark-colored backings in one place too long, especially in front of a glass patio door or anywhere else the sun warms the floor.

Plastic laminates (Formica, etc.). The plastic laminates used on countertops are quite hard and nonporous, but will still absorb some stains. One cure for countertop stains is to simply have patience. A stain like grape juice will look pretty ugly the first day, but will lighten with each successive damp wiping, and will often disappear completely after a few days of regular cleaning. This approach is far preferable to attacking the stain with harsh chemicals, which take their toll on the slick surface of the plastic.

For a stubborn stain, try a poultice of bleaching powdered cleanser such as Ajax or Comet. Mix the cleanser into a paste with water, smear it on the stain, and let it dry. When dry, wipe it up carefully to avoid scratching the plastic, and you'll usually find that the poultice has absorbed the stain. If any remains, repeat the application. (Baking soda and lemon juice will work, too.)

Stubborn stains on plastic laminate can be bleached with a 1:5 mixture of chlorine bleach and water, but don't let it sit on there more than a few minutes. You can also use scouring powder to remove bad stains, but don't get in the habit of scrubbing laminate with abrasive cleansers, colored nylon scrub pads, or steel wool; they'll scratch the surface and make it rough and porous. If you have to use scouring powder to remove a bad stain, be as gentle as possible. If the surface gets scratched from the cleanser, you'll have to restore the finish by polishing it with automotive polishing compound. Coating scratched laminate with appliance wax also helps make it smoother and more stain-resistant. For severe damage like burns or bubbles from cigarettes or hot pans, get a professional countertop installer to "plug" in a new piece.

Fiberglass. We run across fiberglass in everything from motor-boats to drapery fabrics these days, but our biggest concern when it comes to stain removal is usually molded fiberglass tub and shower enclosures, vanity tops, and the like. The mistake we most often make with things like this is scrubbing them with harsh chemicals or abrasive cleansers and colored nylon scrub pads, which make them rough and porous. Then every little speck of hard water, soap scum, or rust that gets on them sinks in or sticks like glue. If you have fiberglass fixtures that have been abused in this way, try restoring the finish by polishing with automotive polishing compound, then coat the surface with a good car wax. This will make the surface smooth and glossy again.

The right approach to take here is to use a white nylon scrub sponge and all-purpose cleaner solution for stubborn spots and stains. If you have to use acid tub and tile cleaners to remove hard-water stains, be sure to rinse the acid away afterward, then wax the surface well to slow down future buildup. Don't use harsh acids like toilet bowl cleaner on fiberglass, and avoid the use of strong solvents such as acetone or lacquer thinner. Oxalic acid solution can be used to remove rust stains, but don't leave it on longer than necessary.

Cultured marble. These "fake marble" vanity tops and sinks are very popular with home builders, but you have to be careful not to damage them in your attempts to clean them. All the instructions given above for fiberglass apply. One advantage of cultured marble is there's no thin finish coat like there is with fiberglass—the material is the same all the way through. So if you get a bad stain or cigarette burn on cultured marble, you can sand it out with 600-grit automotive sandpaper. Wet-sand the damage out, using a light circular motion and plenty of water. Then polish out the sanding scratches with automotive polishing compound and wax the surface. It's time-consuming, but better than buying a new top. Follow the same precautions given for fiberglass as far as stain-removing chemicals are concerned.

Paint and varnish. By this I mean anything—including walls, paneling, furniture, and kitchen cabinets—that has a finish such as paint, varnish, lacquer, shellac or urethane. As you might suspect, there's a great difference in the stain-resistance and cleanability of finishes like these. If your walls are covered with rough, porous, $6.95-a-gallon flat latex paint, don't expect the crayon marks to come off very well. If you had the foresight to apply a good semi-gloss enamel, most stains will stay on the surface where they can be easily wiped away. The big thing to remember with paint and varnish is to not use strong solvents, which can soften or damage the finish. Things like lighter fluid, lacquer thinner, and acetone should not be used on painted surfaces. And you never want to use alcohol on shellac. Paint thinner is okay for removing grease and tar from varnish-type finishes and from enamel paint, but it shouldn't be used on flat latex or left for long on any paint. Use water-based cleaners on flat latex paints, and even then avoid soaking or overaggressive scrubbing—you may end up removing the paint as well.

Avoid scrubbing, scraping, steel wooling, etc., too vigorously on **any** paint or varnish; it could create a dull spot or give you a peek at what the last color was.

Porcelain. This is a slick, hard, glasslike finish, so anything that gets on it is usually just on the surface. It stands up well to most solvents and chemicals, too, so stain removal is generally easy. Two cautions: Don't scrub porcelain tubs, sinks, and appliances with harsh scouring powders—some of them are mean enough to scratch and dull even this tough material. And don't use hydrofluoric acid rust remover (see p. 264) on your porcelain washer top—it'll eat it. Outside of those two things, it's pretty hard to hurt porcelain.

Do be careful of the things that are attached to it, though. Because they themselves are so rugged, we sometimes get carried away when working on porcelain sinks or tubs, and wreak havoc on the metal fittings and surrounding surfaces. Don't use harsh acids like toilet bowl cleaner to remove hard-water stains in porcelain fixtures—they'll damage the chrome drain fittings. Abrasive (colored) nylon scrub pads, too, will scratch chrome. See precautions under Metals for stain-removal chemicals and tools that shouldn't be used on chrome and other bathroom brightwork.

Metals. We tend to think of metals as tough and impenetrable, but they do get stained, and many of them can be damaged by common cleaning and stain-removal chemicals. Softer metals like brass, copper, and silver tarnish readily, and can be prematurely worn out by polishing with abrasive metal-polishing creams. The solvent-impregnated cotton-rope type polishes, such as Ouater (pronounced "water") or Nevr-Dull will be easier on them. Silver or brass or copper that's for display only (not used for food service) should be lacquered to prevent tarnishing. Aluminum, such as anodized window frames, can be lightly oiled with lemon oil and then buffed dry to prevent staining and oxidation.

Chrome is so bright and hard, we often think nothing can hurt it. The truth is, that thin coat of chrome plating on your bathroom faucets or floor lamp is more vulnerable than you imagine. If you have sink drains that used to be bright and shiny chrome but are now a dull brass color or tarnished green, you know what I mean. Scrubbing with abrasive cleansers or colored nylon scrub pads can scratch and dull chrome fixtures. Overenthusiastic rubbing with abrasive metal polishes can wear that shiny surface right away. Harsh acid bowl cleaners or chlorine bleach will eat little pinholes in chrome fixtures, which show up as dark black or green specks.

The best stain-prevention course for chrome is to coat it with appliance wax, then just spray it with window cleaner and polish it with a dry cloth. If it needs polishing, use one of the automotive chrome polishes.

Earth Tile. This includes everything from quarry tile floors to the ceramic tiles used for countertops and shower enclosures. Most of the ceramic tiles, especially those with a shiny glaze, are impervious to just about any stain. The problem, of course, is the grout in between. You can help keep grout from staining by sealing it with a silicone water seal. Apply it liberally to the grout after cleaning, let it soak in, then polish it off the surface of the tiles. If you have "raw" unsealed quarry tile floors, the tile, grout, and all should be sealed with a penetrating masonry seal. Several coats may be necessary to seal the pores completely so stains can't penetrate.

If the grout is already stained, scrub it with a good all-purpose cleaner solution and a stiff brush. Bleaching with a 1:5 dilution of chlorine bleach in water may help, especially for mildew stains in showers (see p. 236). Don't use strong acid masonry cleaners—they eat away the grout cement, and will eventually destroy it.

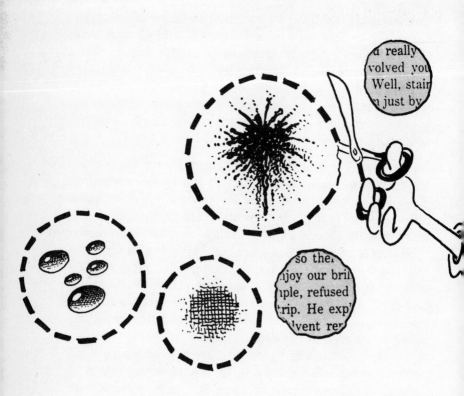

Part III

HOW TO GO ABOUT IT:

The Most Common Spots and Stains and How to Remove Them

Don't let the fancy chemical terms and detailed directions in the following pages intimidate you—taking out most stains is a fairly simple affair. Some of the directions may look involved, but you won't need to do all the steps to take out most stains. Just go from one step to another until the stain is gone, and then you're through! A lot of stains will come out with the first step listed, and only the really tough ones will call for the whole process. Otherwise, there are just a couple of things to remember:

---

1. Take a really good look to make sure you have **all** the stain out before you quit working on it—if there's any left, drying or ironing will probably set it.

---

2. Don't stop right in the middle of a step and leave spotting chemicals in the fabric. If you must stop, go as far as the rinse or flush part of that portion of the instructions, to be sure you get out the last spot remover you used with the recommended rinsing agent before you go off to answer the phone or change that overdue diaper.

---

3. Unless you're putting the object in the wash immediately, always feather the edges of the spotted area as a last step as soon as the stain is gone, whether you've reached the part of the procedure that calls for feathering or not.

To group fabrics in this section according to the stain-removal approach you should use on them I've used the terms "washable" and "dry cleanable." A **washable** fabric means one you would normally launder and that holds up to either hand or machine washing. While many washable fabrics are also dry cleanable, when I use the term dry cleanable here, I mean those fabrics that will tolerate dry cleaning **only**. Within this group you have to use some judgment as to how much water you use in spot removal. Some dry-cleanable fabrics (such as wool) tolerate water fairly well, while others (such as silk or taffeta) can be damaged by using water or wet spotters on them. On any dry-clean-only fabric, the use of water should be limited to sponging the spot or stain for a few minutes and then air drying—never immerse the whole garment or soak it in water. You also want to limit the time any water-based pastes or poultices stay on there to 30 minutes or less.

> For a full explanation of the stain removal techniques specified in this section, see Chapter 4.
>
> For descriptions of the spotting chemicals, see Chapter 5.

To Adapt the Instructions in This Section to Other Surfaces

To make this book as helpful as possible, the stain-removal instructions in the following section are written to apply to the surfaces most commonly stained. Since problem stains occur mostly on clothing, carpeting, and upholstered furniture, most of the procedures focus on stain removal from textiles. And since stain crises really center on clothing, many of the procedures are geared to stain removal in garments. But if a particular stain (such as pet accidents) is more of a concern on carpeting than it is on clothing, the instructions concentrate on carpeting. Stain removal from hard surfaces is described only when it's a special problem or when that's where the stain is mainly found, such as is the case with hard-water stains.

To adapt the instructions in "How to Go About It" to other types of surfaces as well, see Part II. All the chemicals still apply, you just have to adjust the instructions a little here and there to fit the situation.

A Quick Summary of Basic Techniques

Blot. Apply clean white cotton cloths to absorb.

Dry-brush. Brush dry stain matter up and away from the surface lightly with a medium-stiff brush, then vacuum.

Scrape. Slide a scraper back and forth gently over the surface to break up hardened stains, or to help work spotting chemicals in.

Freeze. Apply aerosol gum freeze, dry ice, or ice to the spot to freeze it hard; then fracture it and scrape it away.

Soak. Immerse in water or specified solution for at least 30 minutes. Soak dry cleanables, carpets and upholstery by applying a cloth dampened with the solution.

Poultice. Mix the materials into a paste, apply it to the stain, let it dry, and then wipe it away.

Sponge. Lay the stained article face down on a pad of clean white absorbent cloth and use another such pad, dampened with the spotter, to push the spotter through the stained fabric into the pad below.

Tamp. Spread the stained fabric face up on a smooth level surface and strike the stain firmly with the flat face of a spotting brush.

Flush. Apply the specified liquid liberally to the back side of the stain with a spray or squeeze bottle, to flush it through the fabric.

Rinse. Rinse well with water or the specified solution to remove all stain and spotter residue.

Sponge-rinse. Sponge water through the spot with a clean cloth pad, or in the case of carpeting and upholstery, sponge on clear water and then blot it back out.

Feather. Rinse and dry a spot from the outside in, to blend in the edges and avoid leaving a ring.

STAIN:
Acids

- **WHAT IS IT?** Aggressive acids such as sulfuric, hydrochloric, or muriatic, as found in drain openers, toilet bowl cleaners, and automobile batteries (and in vomit and urine, as well).

- **WHAT CAN IT DO?** The "stain" in this case isn't just the discoloration on the front of your coat where you leaned over your car battery, or the bleached spots where you dribbled bowl cleaner on the bathroom carpet, it's the hole eaten in the fabric that really hurts. Strong acids can damage textiles, metal, marble, and concrete, to say nothing of your skin.

- **HOW HARD?** If you catch it in time there's hope. If you don't, no amount of stain-removal savvy will help, because it's **damage**, not just stain, you'll be dealing with. The key is in recognizing the spill and taking quick action to neutralize it.

- **WHAT TO DO FIRST:** Time is everything with acids. The minute the spill occurs, move as fast as you can. If you get acid on your clothing, the carpet, or your skin, flush the area with plenty of cool water immediately. This will dilute the acid so it can't do its destructive work as quickly. It also gives you time to grab something to neutralize it with. Whatever you do, don't let it dry!

• **WHAT TO DO NEXT**

Fresh: As soon as you've doused it with water, get a strong solution of ammonia or baking soda on the spill to neutralize the acid. Once you get the neutralizer on, you don't have to be in such a rush—it won't hurt anything now. Blot out the neutralizer solution, then rinse and blot several times with clear water. If it's a hard surface, rinse well after neutralizing. If it's washable, then launder it; take dry cleanables in for cleaning.

Old/Dry: If you've spilled acid on your clothes without realizing it, you usually find out when you wash them—they come out of the laundry with holes in them! Once the acid has dried, it's usually too late. But if you know you've spilled acid on something and it's dried, don't just throw it in the washer—the water will just activate the acid and allow it to do more dirty work. The damage may already be done, but maybe not. Before you get the object wet, apply a neutralizer solution to stop the action of the acid, then go ahead and launder it. For dry cleanables, just take it in dry and let the cleaner know about the stain, but don't count on removal.

• **IF THAT DOESN'T DO IT:** Wear that shirt when you fix the car or paint the bedroom.

• **CAUTION:** Stay away from strong acids—they're not only dangerous to your clothes and furnishings, but to you, too. Even weak acids like vinegar and urine can cause color changes in some dyes and weaken cotton and linen.

• **PREVENTION:** Follow the directions when using drain openers—don't just dump in half the bottle and let 'er boil. Don't wave your swab around anywhere or carry a dripping swab across the carpet when you're using bowl cleaner, and don't set a wet bottle of bowl cleaner on anything, and that includes the sink.

Acne Medications (see Chemical Stains, p. 88)

STAIN:
Adhesives
(gummy adhesives—
not glue or chewing gum)

• **WHAT IS IT?** The stickum from adhesive, cellophane, strapping, and other tapes, which is often left behind when the tape is removed or a Band-Aid is walked into the carpet, etc. There's lots of adhesive, too, in those labels and stickers that are somewhere on almost everything we buy.

• **WHAT CAN IT DO?** Stick to the surface, and get harder and more firmly bonded to it with time, heat, sunlight, and pressure. These gooey spots also attract dirt and lint.

• **HOW HARD?** Fairly easy when fresh; a mighty sticky job if you leave it to dry out and harden.

• **WHAT TO DO FIRST:** Peel off any remaining tape or sticker, and remove as much of the gummy deposit as possible.

Gently scraping with a fingernail works safely on most surfaces, but on fabric, you have to be careful not to drive the adhesive deeper into the weave. Plucking it off is safer for fabrics than scraping. On hard surfaces, the adhesive can often be rolled into balls with the thumb and lifted off.

- **WHAT TO DO NEXT**
Fresh: Sponge on **dry spotter** with a soft cloth, and loosen and lift off the adhesive as the solvent softens it. Be careful not to rub dissolved adhesive further into fabrics. Remove the last traces of adhesive by gently rubbing and blotting with a clean cloth and the spotter.
Old/Dry: Put a pad moistened with dry spotter over the stain and keep it moistened with solvent so it doesn't dry out. (Covering it with Saran wrap can help here.) Leave it on until the spot is soft, then proceed as above.

- **IF THAT DOESN'T DO IT:** Dry cleaning solvents won't remove all adhesives easily. If the dry spotter doesn't soften it, use an orange-oil solvent such as De-Solv-it. This will loosen most adhesives, and works like magic on hard surfaces. If you use it on fabric, after the adhesive is gone the orange-oil solvent needs to be flushed with dry spotter or laundered, or it will leave an oily stain.

- **CAUTION:** If you're using De-Solv-it on carpeting, use it sparingly. If you slosh it on, it'll sink down into the depths of the carpet where it's hard to get out, and keep wicking up to the surface to create a dirt-attracting, oily stain.

- **PREVENTION:** Remember that it's a lot easier to apply tape than it is to get it off—pay attention to where you're putting it and don't use too much "extra." Pick up that stray sticker or shed Band-Aid as soon as you see it.

---

antiperspirant stains (see Perspiration)
apple (see Fruit—Clear)

STAIN:
Baby Food/
Baby Formula

- **WHAT IS IT?** Vegetables, fruits, proteins, soya, synthetic compounds, usually blended with plenty of precious little drools.

- **WHAT CAN IT DO?** Some of the fruit and vegetable stains, especially, can be dark and noticeable enough to ruin rompers or buntings if allowed to set. And the combination of fruit, sugar, and other ingredients can easily be set by washing in hot water, soap, ironing, or by hot-air drying.

- **HOW HARD?** Usually manageable if treated while fresh. Left to dry, some of the fruit stains can become a real problem (especially the ones that end up on the ceiling!).

- **WHAT TO DO FIRST:** Scrape off as much as you can and blot up any liquid.

- **WHAT TO DO NEXT**
  Fresh: For baby's clothes (washable, we hope), soak immediately in **digestant** for 30 minutes to an hour and then

launder. For the stray spot on mom or dad's dry-cleanable clothing or on carpet and upholstery, sponge with wet spotter, then rinse with water, feather, and air dry. If stain remains, sponge with dry spotter.

Old/Dry: Washables: Soak overnight in cool water, and wring out. Spray the stain with laundry pre-treat, then wash with a bleach safe for the fabric and warm water. Dry cleanables: Sponge first with wet spotter, then with dry spotter; rinse and feather.

• **IF THAT DOESN'T DO IT:** Switching babies doesn't usually do any good, but repeated launderings will often lighten or remove any remaining stains.

• **CAUTION:** Don't use ammonia or other strong alkaline cleaners, or apply heat, either of which will set fruit and sugar stains.

• **PREVENTION:** Don't leave half-empty baby bottles lying anywhere, and buy a bigger bib!

---

ballpoint pen (see Ink—Ballpoint)

barbecue sauce (see Catsup and Fast Food Stains)

STAIN:
Beer

- **WHAT IS IT?** Water, alcohol, sugar, protein—a combination stain.

- **WHAT CAN IT DO?** The alcohol in beer can "burn" woolens (turn them dark and brittle), and oxidize on any fabric to form a permanent stain; sugar stains can become permanent with heat; the protein will produce that unmistakable stale-beer smell.

- **HOW HARD?** Because the combination of ingredients, requires several steps to remove. Should be no problem if caught when fresh, but a dried-on stain can be difficult, an ironed-on one impossible.

- **WHAT TO DO FIRST:** Don't let it dry. Blot up all you can, and sponge the spot with a mild **vinegar** solution, or at least with water.

- **WHAT TO DO NEXT**
  Fresh: After vinegar sponging, rinse with lukewarm water. Apply digestant paste and let it sit for 30 minutes without drying out. Rinse with lukewarm water. Launder washables in warm water as soon as possible.
  Old/Dry: For washables, soak the garment in cool water overnight, then treat as above. Take dry cleanable garments in for expert spotting and cleaning.

• **IF THAT DOESN'T DO IT:** Bleach with a mild bleach (see p. 32-34). If the alcohol has caused the dye to bleed or run, there's no fixing it.

• **CAUTION:** Don't iron a beer stain or dry it with hot air unless you're absolutely sure it's gone—heat can make it permanent.

• **PREVENTION:** Take it easy when you're tipping the can to get that last drop, and remember that cans and bottles (rolling on car floors, in garbage cans, under the bleachers, on the right of way, wherever) usually still contain a last little bit of beer.

Big Mac Stains (see Catsup and Fast Food Stains)
black marks on floors (see Heel Marks)
blackberry (see Fruit—Red)

STAIN:
Bleach

• **WHAT IS IT?** A number of things can bleach fabrics (see p. 32-34). The most common cause of unwanted white or light spots on clothing and carpeting is liquid chlorine bleach (such as Clorox or Purex). Whatever the cause, the treatment is the same.

• **WHAT CAN IT DO?** Make you a blonde, and strip the color out of fabric and other surfaces.

• **HOW HARD?** The worst.

• **WHAT TO DO FIRST:** If you get bleach on something accidentally, or notice a color change in something you're spotting, flood the area with cool water immediately.

• **WHAT TO DO NEXT**
Fresh: Flooding it with water is all you can do. If you get it diluted quickly enough, the color change may be slight enough to be unnoticeable. If not, sayonara, sexy slacks.
Old/Dry: Sorry. Once the dye is bleached out of a fabric, there's no way of reversing the process. Not even tears will neutralize it. Bleached spots in carpeting can sometimes be re-dyed by expert carpet dyers to more or less match the surrounding material, but there's no way you're going to reconstruct the pattern on your paisley blouse.

• **IF THAT DOESN'T DO IT:** Wear it to weed the garden, or wait until the tie-dyed look returns.

• **PREVENTION:** Think twice about using chlorine bleach —it isn't the wonder drug for whites we used to think it was. Most savvy launderers only use chlorine bleach occasionally, because of its ability to weaken and deteriorate fabrics. Be very careful when storing and using chlorine bleach—always let the washer fill first, then add the bleach and make sure it's well mixed with the water before adding clothes.

• **PREVENTION:** Don't wear your favorite flannel shirt while applying the mildew killer, and always handle bleach solutions like the dangerous liquids they are—don't splash or slosh them around.

STAIN:
Blood

- **WHAT IS IT?** Protein, mineral salts, water.

- **WHAT CAN IT DO?** Leave a faint permanent "rust" stain if allowed to set. (Fresh bloodstains can at least get you a little pity and attention.)

- **HOW HARD?** When fresh, it's easy to remove. Can be a real challenge when dried and set.

- **WHAT TO DO FIRST:** Keep the stain wet! Blot out any fresh blood, then put washables to soak in cold salt water, or rinse out under the cold-water tap. For dry cleanables, carpets, and mattresses, sponge cold water onto the spot.

- **WHAT TO DO NEXT**
  Fresh: Without letting the spot dry, launder washable items in a regular cold-water wash. For dry cleanables, sponge with cold water to which you've added a few drops of ammonia,

then flush thoroughly with cold water. (No ammonia on silk or wool!)

Old/Dry: For washable fabrics, soak in cool salt water for several hours and rinse thoroughly. Soak again in cool water to which you've added several tablespoons of ammonia, then wash as above. For dry cleanables, sponge with salt water and treat as above.

Bloodstains often get on mattresses, pillows, upholstery, etc. Treat these according to instructions on p. 143-148.

• **IF THAT DOESN'T DO IT:** Soak in digestant for 30 minutes to an hour or moisten with digestant paste for 30 minutes, but don't let it dry out; then rinse. Don't use digestant on wool or silk. If stain still remains, bleach with hydrogen peroxide and rinse. If you haven't got rid of it yet, apply rust remover. If stain still remains, use as strong a bleach as the fabric will tolerate.

• **CAUTION:** Don't let the stain dry out before you've got it beat—dry blood is much more difficult to remove. Don't hot-air dry or iron until you're sure it's gone. Don't use vinegar—acids will set bloodstains.

• **PREVENTION:** Don't just stick a piece of toilet paper over that shaving cut near your collar and hope for the best. And put a bandage on that cut finger instead of walking all over the house holding it out or against your hip.

---

blueberry (see Fruit—Red)

blusher (see Makeup)

bowl cleaner (see Acid)

butter (see Greasy Foods)

candle wax (see Wax)

STAIN:
Candy
(other than chocolate)

- **WHAT IS IT?** Sugar, flavorings, dyes.

- **WHAT CAN IT DO?** Attract ants, and the dyes used to color candies can make some permanent stains. A sugar stain, if accidentally ironed, also makes a nasty yellow-brown spot.

- **HOW HARD?** Easy, unless dye-stained or heat-set.

- **WHAT TO DO FIRST:** Pry the kid from it first, then scrape or pluck all you can from the surface.

- **WHAT TO DO NEXT**
  Fresh: For washables, soaking or laundering in warm water will usually remove candy stains. For dry-cleanables, carpet, and the like, sponge first with warm water, then with wet spotter and a few drops of vinegar. Finish by sponge-rinsing with water and feathering.
  Old/Dry: If that Gummy Bear is glued to the fabric, dampen with warm neutral detergent solution and allow candy to soften before removing, to avoid pulling fibers loose or injuring other surfaces.

- **IF THAT DOESN'T DO IT:** For washables, apply laundry pre-treat and launder in warm water. For dry cleanables, sponge with alcohol (no alcohol on acetate, and pretest other fabrics for dye change first), then sponge-rinse with water.

• **CAUTION:** Be sure all traces of the sugar are gone before ironing or hot-air drying.

• **PREVENTION:** Don't serve anything that can be half eaten, then slipped under the couch cushion or onto the windowsill.

Sweets for the Neat

If you've reached the end of your licorice rope and never want another peppermint holding the couch cushions in place, or the thought of Nerds crushed in your carpet pile makes you shudder, ban your brood to the backyard for snacks!

There are more- and less-messy candies, so choose wisely and you won't end up the all-day sucker. Ask any mom and she'll tell you: Smarties over taffy; one-bite size over a bar of anything; avoid any candy that squirts, turns your hands or mouth green, or is granular. Pass over the Easter Peeps, too, or anything marshmallow. Don't forget that no one's ever eaten an entire Sugar Daddy in one sitting, or successfully sued the "melt in your mouthers" for damage to their car seats. If you pass out five Tootsie-Roll Pops, demand to get five sticks in return. And don't stand in front of the gumball machine (with the kids in dress whites) thinking, "What can it hurt?" You know four nickels in a row will turn out four bright color-me-blue gumballs.

STAIN:
Carbon Paper, Typewriter/ Printer Ribbon, Newspaper Ink

- **WHAT IS IT?** Ink (dye), bonded to a ribbon, sheet, etc.

- **WHAT CAN IT DO?** Rub off on clothing, carpet, furniture, and hands, leaving a dark smudge.

- **HOW HARD?** Inked ribbons can leave a pretty tough stain; carbon paper isn't too bad; newsprint is fairly easy.

- **WHAT TO DO FIRST:** If it's on your hands, wash them before touching your clothing or scratching your nose. If it's on your clothes, don't rub it! Follow the steps below and blot **gently** to avoid spreading the stain and driving it deeper in.

- **WHAT TO DO NEXT**
  Washables: Blot with dry spotter until no more ink is being removed, then apply laundry pre-treat and launder in warm water. Air dry.
  Dry Cleanables: Blot with dry spotter until no more ink is being removed, and let dry. If stain remains, sponge with ammonia (no ammonia on silk or wool), then with wet spotter; rinse and feather.

Hands: Thanks to the oils in our skin, many inks will wash off with soap and water. If stain doesn't come off easily, rub in hand lotion, leave it on there a while and then wash.

• **IF THAT DOESN'T DO IT:** Bleach with as strong a bleach as the fabric will tolerate.

• **PREVENTION:** Use the plastic gloves that come with the ribbon, and quit trying to change ribbons while you're on the phone!

STAIN:
Catsup, Spaghetti Sauce, Barbecue Sauce, Steak Sauce

• **WHAT IS IT?** Tomato, sugar, tannin, seasoning, possibly oil, maybe coloring.

• **WHAT CAN IT DO?** Season any style of clothes you own with a reddish-brown stain that will set with heat.

• **HOW HARD?** Takes some doing even when fresh; can become permanent if heat-set.

- **WHAT TO DO FIRST:** Scrape and then blot to remove residue.

- **WHAT TO DO NEXT**

  Fresh: Washables: Sponge with cool water. Apply laundry pre-treat, tamp if the fabric will tolerate it, and rinse. If stain is gone, launder in warm water. If stain remains, sponge with a solution of half vinegar and half water, and rinse again. Reapply laundry pre-treat and wash in warm water. Dry Cleanables: Sponge with cool water and let dry. Sponge with dry spotter. If stain remains, sponge with solution of half vinegar and half water, then rinse.

  Old/Dry: Soften stain with warm glycerin and treat as above.

- **IF THAT DOESN'T DO IT:** Soak washables in digestant 30 minutes to an hour and rewash. Apply digestant paste to dry cleanables, let it sit 30 minutes without drying out, then rinse. As a last resort, bleach with hydrogen peroxide.

- **CAUTION:** Don't use hot water, dry with heat, or iron until the stain is gone—heat will set it.

- **PREVENTION:** Trade in that slow catsup so you won't have to beat on the bottle and splatter it around; don't put a puddle on your plate three times larger than you could ever consume. And when in Rome, wear a bib!

cherry (see Fruit—Red)

STAIN:
Chocolate (chocolate
candy, cocoa, chocolate ice cream)

- **WHAT IS IT?** Fats, protein, sugar (and a hard-to-break habit).

- **WHAT CAN IT DO?** Make a messy brown stain that spreads easily and will oxidize and set with age and heat.

- **HOW HARD?** The combination of ingredients calls for a multi-method attack, but it's a fairly easy stain to remove when fresh.

- **WHAT TO DO FIRST:** Take one last sniff, then scrape or blot up all you can, being careful not to push it farther into the fabric. And watch where you scrape it **to**, or you'll have a second spot.

- **WHAT TO DO NEXT**
Fresh: After scraping and blotting, apply absorbent to soak up as much of the remaining grease as possible. Remove the absorbent and sponge the stain with dry spotter, and keep on working spotter through the fabric and into the blotter until no more color is being transferred. Any remaining stain will be the protein. Soak washables for 30 minutes to an hour in digestant, and launder in warm water. Use digestant paste on dry cleanables except for wool or silk, but don't let it dry out; then sponge-rinse with cool water.
Old/Dry: Same as above, if stain has not been hot-air dried or ironed.

- **IF THAT DOESN'T DO IT:** Washables: Use a bleach safe for the fabric and launder. Dry cleanables: Try hydrogen peroxide. If stain is set and will not respond, take in for professional spotting.

- **CAUTION:** Be sure all traces of the stain are gone before ironing or hot-air drying, as this will set it.

- **PREVENTION:** Eschew chocolate fondue, make sure you've stopped shivering **before** you lift the cocoa to your lips; provide a discreet disposal container beside the Grand Deluxe Assortment for the "bite-and-rejects."

STAIN:
Cigarette Burns

- **WHAT IS IT?** Once in a while it's just nicotine and tar residues, which can be removed by spot cleaning. Usually, though, there's scorching and some charring of the fiber or surface.

- **WHAT CAN IT DO?** Anything from slight discoloration to a gaping hole.

- **HOW HARD?** The worst.

- **WHAT TO DO FIRST:** Find out how bad it is. Is there actual damage to the fiber or surface, or just heat darkening? Work to remove any black or yellow-brown discoloration first, so you can assess the situation.

- **WHAT TO DO NEXT**

Garments: If there's a hole burned in an everyday garment, give it up—relegate it to the ragbag or the work clothes closet. If it's an exotic, expensive, or hopelessly sentimental item, consult an expert to see if reweaving can save it. If it's just discolored, launder it in hot water with chlorine bleach, if safe for the fabric. Sponge dry cleanables with neutral detergent solution and rinse.

Carpet and Upholstery: Camouflage is what we want to accomplish here—to blend the burn in with the surrounding area as much as possible. Lightly rub the burn with medium steel wool first. This will remove a lot of the char and lighten the color considerably. Then vacuum up the debris. Spot clean with neutral detergent solution and rinse.

Blackened or melted carpet tufts can be snipped off with scissors and new tufts from a closet or out-of-the-way place glued in with hot glue or white glue to fill any bald areas. After the glue is well set, brush the new tufts up straight and give them a uniform haircut. If it's a bad burn, a carpet repairman can cut the damaged section out and replace ("plug") it with a piece cut from your remnant or from a closet.

About all you can do with bad burns in upholstery is replace the damaged panel or re-cover the whole piece.

Hard Surfaces: Burns in wood can be spot-stripped with paint and varnish remover, sanded out, then refinished with paint or stain and varnish. Slight burns in plastic laminate such as Formica can be removed with scouring powder, then the surface polished back to a shine with automotive polishing compound. The same treatment will help fiberglass and vinyl flooring. Severe burns in Formica or plastic surfaces call for patching in a new piece or complete replacement.

• **PREVENTION:** Learn to use the ash tray or give up smoking. Don't set a lighted cigarette **anywhere** "for a minute." Aslett 12:14: That which is set down will be forgotten.

cocoa (see Chocolate)

STAIN:
Coffee/Tea

• **WHAT IS IT?** Tannin, protein, maybe sugar and animal fat (cream) or nondairy creamer.

• **WHAT CAN IT DO?** A coffee spill will leave a yellowish-brown stain that can be hard to remove, especially if there was sugar in it and it has been ironed. Old, set coffee is worse than cold coffee!

• **HOW HARD?** Usually manageable when fresh, difficult if set and especially if ironed. Can be a real problem on light-colored wool or cotton. If it was "coffee with" (cream and/or sugar), the combination of ingredients calls for a multi-method approach, and may require more than one attempt.

• **WHAT TO DO FIRST:** Act immediately—don't let it dry out. Blot up all you can with a clean cloth, and sponge with cool water as long as any stain is coming out.

• **WHAT TO DO NEXT**

Fresh: Washables: Apply laundry pre-treat and launder in warm water—air dry. Dry Cleanables: Sponge with wet spotter and a few drops of vinegar, then flush with cool water (except for water-sensitive fabrics) and feather.

Old/Dry: Washables: Treat same as Fresh stain. Dry cleanables: smear stain with glycerin, let it sit 30 minutes, then treat as for Fresh stain.

• **IF THAT DOESN'T DO IT:**   For washables, soak in digestant for 30 minutes to an hour and launder in warm water and then air dry. For dry cleanables, apply digestant paste; keep it on for 30 minutes and don't let it dry out; rinse. (No digestant on silk or wool.) For wool, apply glycerin, let it sit 30 minutes, and sponge off with water. Stains may require final spotting with dry spotter if the coffee or tea had cream in it. Any remaining stain should be bleached with hydrogen peroxide for bleach-sensitive fabrics, or with chlorine bleach if safe (test first).

• **CAUTION:**   Don't use ammonia or heat—it can set a coffee stain. And don't be drinking another cup while removing this one!

• **PREVENTION:**   Don't carry uncovered cups of coffee; it doesn't matter **how** carefully you carry it—if you move too fast it'll slosh. Never set your cup on the floor, even for a minute. If you insist on drinking in vehicles, don't make light of commuter mugs. And in case you wondered why saucers were invented, it was to catch spills and make sure there'd always be somewhere to set dripping spoons.

---

cola (see Soft Drinks)

collar rings (see Chapter 2)

cologne (see Perfume)
contact cement (see Glue—Synthetic)
corn syrup (see Honey)

STAIN:
Correction Fluid
(such as Liquid Paper)

• **WHAT IS IT?** A solvent-based opaque coating (essentially just a fast-drying paint).

• **WHAT CAN IT DO?** Leave a highly visible spot that resists laundering.

• **HOW HARD?** Not too bad on fabrics that tolerate acetone. Can be hard to remove from delicate fabrics.

• **WHAT TO DO FIRST:** Gently flake or scrape off as much as possible, being careful not to damage the fabric. Flexing the fabric before you scrape will usually help to break up the hardened spots.

• **WHAT TO DO NEXT**
Delicate Fabrics (acetate, triacetate, rayon, silk, and wool): Take to a professional cleaner for expert spotting and cleaning.

Durable Fabrics: Sponge with acetone (test first). Gently scrape or tamp to loosen the hardened film as you sponge with the solvent. When the stain is removed, flush with neutral detergent solution and rinse with water.

• **IF THAT DOESN'T DO IT:** Use water-rinseable paint and varnish remover (test first). Scrape or tamp to loosen the film as the solvent softens it, then rinse with water. Repeat as necessary.

CAUTION: Don't pluck hardened correction fluid off fabric—it can pull and tear the fibers. Flex and scrape to break up the film before trying to pull it off.

• **PREVENTION:** Let it **dry** not only before you try to write or type on it, but before you run it through the typewriter roller or lean your hand or arm or sleeve on it. Keep the bottle close to the booboo zone so you don't have to carry a dripping brush any distance, and take the two seconds it takes at bottle top to wipe off brush overload.

---

cranberry (see Fruit—Red)

crayons (see Wax)

cream (see Milk)

drain opener (If Acid-type drain opener, see Acid. If Lye-type opener, see Oven Cleaner)

STAIN:
Dye

• **WHAT IS IT?** Food colorings, Easter egg dye, hair coloring, dye transferred from dark colors in laundry, from meat labels, etc.

• **WHAT CAN IT DO?** Dyes are designed to stain, and most of them are not meant to be removed. Dyes can leave permanent stains, even when caught quickly and handled flawlessly, but many times they can be removed.

• **HOW HARD?** The worst.

• **WHAT TO DO FIRST:** Act fast—don't let it dry out. Put washables to soak in cool water and sponge off dry cleanables. Blot up colored drink stains as fast as you can and neutralize them immediately as per Kool-Aid, p. 226-227.

• **WHAT TO DO NEXT**
Red: Red is the least colorfast of all dyes—we've all had "pink loads" where a red garment has bled color onto a washer

load of whites. This can happen with other dark colors, too. For instructions on handling this problem, see p. 41.

Soak washables for 30 minutes to an hour in a quart of water to which you've added one-half teaspoon laundry detergent and two tablespoons of ammonia. Rinse, apply laundry pre-treat, and keep it wet 20 minutes, then launder in cool water with a bleach safe for the fabric. If color remains, use color remover; test first.

For red dye stains on dry-cleanable clothing, carpets, and upholstery, the safest course is to let a professional cleaner handle it. If you're dead set on doing it yourself, first sponge with dry spotter, then with a wet spotter and a few drops of ammonia. Keep sponging the wet spotter and ammonia through the stain into a clean cloth until no more color is being removed. (Go easy on the ammonia for silk and wool.) Flush with cool water, then sponge with a mild vinegar solution and let dry. If color remains, use color remover; test first.

- **IF THAT DOESN'T DO IT:**
  If you have what seems like a hopeless red Kool-Aid, Popsicle, or Jell-O stain in carpeting, professional carpet cleaners have specialized products that can remove it.

  Yellow: Sponge with dry spotter until no more color is being removed. If color remains, apply amyl acetate, tamp, flush with dry spotter, and let dry. If it's still there, sponge with a mixture of half water, half alcohol, and a few drops of vinegar; test for colorfastness first—dilute alcohol for acetate or rayon, no vinegar on cotton or linen. Rinse.

  All other colors: Washables: Soak for 30 minutes to an hour in one quart of water to which you've added one-half teaspoon laundry detergent and two tablespoons vinegar; substitute ammonia for vinegar if fabric is cotton or linen. Rinse, soak in digestant for 30 minutes to an hour, and launder in warm water. If stain remains, sponge with water/alcohol/vinegar solution, as for Yellow (follow fabric precautions), and rinse.

Dry cleanables: Sponge with dry spotter until no more color is being removed, then with wet spotter along with a few drops of vinegar, and rinse with cool water. If stain remains, try the water/alcohol/vinegar procedure under Yellow (including all fabric precautions), rinse, and feather.

• **PREVENTION:** Resist the urge to throw something else into "all that wasted space" when the label tells you to wash it separately the first time. To be on the safe side run that hot pink jogging suit through solo the second time, too.

Don't set the ground-round wrapper on the counter—put it right in the trash.

STAIN:
Egg

• **WHAT IS IT?** Protein (albumin), fat, salts, water.

• **WHAT CAN IT DO?** Leave you with egg on more than your face. If set by heat, can be permanent. Can also do serious damage to painted surfaces, including house siding and yes, vehicle finishes.

• **HOW HARD?** Easy, if caught quickly.

• **WHAT TO DO FIRST:** Gently scrape up all you can.

• **WHAT TO DO NEXT**

Washables: Soak in digestant for 30 minutes to an hour and wash in warm water. Air dry. If oily stain remains, sponge with dry spotter.

Dry Cleanables: Apply digestant paste; leave it on for 30 minutes without drying out, then rinse with warm water. If stain remains, sponge with wet spotter and a few drops of ammonia (no ammonia on silk or wool). Rinse, feather, and air dry. If oily stain remains, sponge with dry spotter.

Hard Surfaces: Wash it off immediately with plenty of cool neutral detergent solution.

• **IF THAT DOESN'T DO IT:** Use the strongest bleach safe for the fabric.

• **CAUTION:** Don't use hot water or hot-air drying—heat will set egg stains!

• **PREVENTION:** Don't order soft-boiled eggs at power breakfasts. Don't carry dripping shells across the carpet. Don't make the neighborhood kids mad at you right before Halloween.

epoxy (see Glue—Synthetic)

eye shadow (see Makeup)

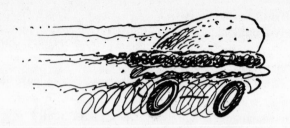

STAIN:
Fast Food Stains

- **WHAT IS IT?** Usually a greasy stain from a dropped french fry, a dripping burger, or a bit of dribbled soup and sandwich at lunch. Occasionally a more serious attack of Big Mac sauce or barbecue goo.

- **WHAT CAN IT DO?** Make you look like an idiot for the rest of the day. (If left for any length of time, these can also be hard to remove.)

- **HOW HARD?** Catsup and tartar sauce splotches can get a little complicated, but the simple grease spots are easy. You just need to keep a thing or two on hand and know what to do.

- **WHAT TO DO FIRST:** If it's just on the car seat, sponge it with water and leave it until you get home. If it's all down your front, get a plastic spoon and head for the restroom. You can use a credit card if nothing else is available. Scrape off whatever you can and use toilet paper to blot (don't rub!) away as much of the grease as possible. Then go to your car, purse, or desk drawer, and get out the spray can of dry spotter you keep handy for just such occasions.

• **WHAT TO DO NEXT**

Grease Spots (Meat juice, deep-fried foods, potato chips, mayonnaise, salad dressing, etc.): For light stains, just spray a little dry spotter on a clean white handkerchief and gently rub out the spot, feathering the edge as you finish. For heavier spots, you'll have to put an absorbent pad of paper toweling behind the stain, spray the spotter directly onto the spot, then sponge it through with the handkerchief. Continue until the grease is gone, then feather out the edge. (In a pinch, you can use paper towels instead of a hanky, but it'll leave the stain site clearly outlined in lint.)

Water and Sugar-Based Stains (Soft drinks, juice, coffee, etc.): Sponge off the spot with plain cool water. If it doesn't come entirely out, fight off the urge to use the hand soap in the restroom on it—this can set fruit stains. Do the best you can with water and wait until you can get your hands on some wet spotter and maybe some vinegar. Feather out the wet edges with a dry towel to avoid leaving a ring.

Combination Stains (Hamburger sauce, barbecue sauce, etc.): Sponge first with the dry spotter, then with cool water and a dab of hand soap (no soap on fruit stains). Feather the edge as you finish. If a ring remains when dry, sponge with the dry spotter.

• **CAUTION:** This is first aid or emergency procedure only— don't forget to take proper care of the stain when you get home. Don't hot-air dry or iron the item before the stain is gone.

• **PREVENTION:** Bear in mind that "To Gos" have blotched a lot more garments than "To Stays." Don't order Big Macs when you're immaculate. Keep your hand out of the bag till you get back home/to the office. Use the sixteen napkins you took. And when scanning menus, remember that cheese glops and sauces drip and tomato slips out.

---

feces, animal or human (see Pet Stains)

felt-tip markers (see Ink—Felt-tip markers)

food coloring (see Dye)

french fries (see Fast Food Stains and Greasy Foods)

STAIN:
Fruit—Clear (light-colored fruits such as apple, pear, orange, lemon, lime, or grapefruit, either fresh fruit or fruit juice)

- **WHAT IS IT?** Fruit and sugar.

- **WHAT CAN IT DO?** Almost invisible when fresh, clear fruit spots can turn into ugly yellowish-brown stains if you let them go, because of the sugar in them.

- **HOW HARD?** Easy if treated when fresh; hard or impossible if set by age and heat, especially on light-colored wool. Once a sugar stain's been ironed, it's ornery!

- **WHAT TO DO FIRST:** Don't ignore clear fruit stains just because they don't look like much. Treat any spills immediately by first blotting up any liquid and scraping away any solids, and then sponging thoroughly with cool water.

• **WHAT TO DO NEXT**
Fresh: Washables: If color is still visible after the initial water rinse, sponge with wet spotter and a few drops of vinegar, then apply pre-treat and launder. If stain still remains, soak in digestant up to an hour and launder.

Dry Cleanables:: Sponge thoroughly with wet spotter and a few drops of vinegar, then rinse with cool water. If stain remains, apply a digestant paste, let it sit for 30 minutes without drying out, then rinse with water.

Old/Dry: Rub glycerin into the stain to soften it, then treat as above. If the stain has been ironed, it may be permanent.

• **IF THAT DOESN'T DO IT:** Bleach with as strong a bleach as the fabric will tolerate.

• **CAUTION:** Don't launder in hot water. Don't use real soap (such as bar soap, Ivory Snow, Woolite)—it will set fruit stains. Don't use heat, such as hot-air drying or ironing, until the stain is completely gone. Remember that fresh fruit doesn't just drip—it crunches, spurts, and squirts—so don't be too quick to conclude you've got it all.

• **PREVENTION:** Don't eat navel oranges on the new couch. Don't wipe your hands on your apron, your best tea towel, or the back of your slacks when you're making fruit salad or canning peaches.

STAIN:

Fruit—Red (red or deeply colored fruits such as cherry, grape, blueberry, blackberry, cranberry, or raspberry, either fresh fruit or fruit juice)

• **WHAT IS IT?** Fruit, sugar (and one of the easiest stains to see).

• **WHAT CAN IT DO?** Make you abandon your plans for a berry farm. The strong red dyes can also leave permanent stains, and the sugar will turn yellow with age and heat.

• **HOW HARD?** Manageable to impossible, depending on the fruit and the fabric.

• **WHAT TO DO FIRST:** Treating it while it's still fresh is critical—the sooner the better. First scrape and blot up all you can, then immediately and repeatedly sponge with cool water until no more color is being removed. For cotton, linen, and other sturdy white or colorfast fabrics, consider using the boiling water method below. For other fabrics, use the gentler procedures.

• **WHAT TO DO NEXT**
Boiling Water Method: This works surprisingly well for removing fruit stains, but it must be used cautiously, and only on fresh stains. Only sturdy, colorfast fabrics (such as white or colorfast cotton and linen) that can tolerate boiling water should be considered. Pretesting is always wise to avoid fabric damage. Stretch the stained fabric, face down, over a large bowl and secure it with a rubber band. Put the bowl in the bathtub, so nothing can spatter on you. Pour a quart of boiling water through the stain from a height of two to three feet. Yes, heat sets stains, but with this method the flow of hot water flushes the stain out of the fabric before it can adhere. If a stain remains after this, or if the fabric won't tolerate boiling water, go to the following procedures.

Washables: Sponge with lemon juice or rub a freshly cut lemon into the stain. Rinse with water, blot out all the moisture you can, and let it air dry the rest of the way. If stain remains, sponge with wet spotter and a few drops of vinegar. (Dilute vinegar with two parts water for use on cotton or linen.) Tamp while sponging if the fabric will tolerate it. Apply laundry pretreat and launder in warm water. If the stain remains, soak in digestant for 30 minutes to an hour and relaunder.

Dry Cleanables: Follow procedure for washables down through the lemon juice, wet spotter with vinegar, and tamping. Rinse with cool water. If stain remains, apply a digestant paste, let it sit for 30 minutes without drying out, then rinse with water.

Old/Dry: Rub glycerin into the stain to soften it, then treat as above. If the stain has been ironed, it may be permanent. Old stains on valuable pieces should be taken in for expert spotting.

• **IF THAT DOESN'T DO IT:** Bleach with as strong a bleach as the fabric will tolerate.

• **CAUTION:** Don't launder in hot water. Don't use real soap—it will set fruit stains. Don't use heat (other than the boiling water method) such as hot-air drying or ironing until the stain is completely gone.

• **PREVENTION:** Don't try to eat berry anything without a dish, spoon, and napkin. Don't wipe your hands on your pants when you're picking, and watch that juice when you're washing, hulling, cutting or transporting these tasty little morsels.

fruit syrup (see Jam)

STAIN:
Furniture Polish

• **WHAT IS IT?** Oil; possibly dyes, waxes, or silicone.

• **WHAT CAN IT DO?** Dampen your enthusiasm for shiny shelves. Most polishes will make an oily stain, and the dyes in colored polishes can leave a permanent stain. Some polishes will also alter red carpet dyes, creating a green or bluish halo around the base of polished furniture.

• **HOW HARD?** The darker, the more dangerous. The plain oily stain isn't too bad; dark-colored dye stains (like dark walnut scratch cover) can be tough.

• **WHAT TO DO FIRST:** Quickly apply an absorbent, and leave it on until as much of the oil as possible is absorbed; this may take several hours.

• **WHAT TO DO NEXT**
Fresh: After absorbing as much oil as possible, remove the absorbent and sponge with dry spotter. Keep sponging with fresh spotter and blotting until all the oil is removed. For washables, apply laundry pre-treat and launder in warm water.

Old/Dry: For washables, apply laundry pre-treat and rub in some petroleum jelly, let it sit 15 minutes, and launder in warm water. For dry cleanables, rub in petroleum jelly, let it sit 15 minutes, and then sponge thoroughly with dry spotter.

• **IF THAT DOESN'T DO IT:** Allow the spot to dry. Sponge with wet spotter and a few drops of vinegar, flush with water (no vinegar on cotton or linen). If dye stain remains, treat as for Dye, p. 188-190.

• **CAUTION:** Oil stains will oxidize and become hard to remove after a few days, and even faster in the presence of heat—so treat as quickly as possible.

• **PREVENTION:** Pay attention to where you're setting the polish bottle (and for that matter, your oily rag). And don't get an aerosol unless you have tight control of your trigger finger.

STAIN:
Glue—
Synthetic
(Super Glue, hot melt, epoxy resin, plastic model cement, clear household cement, etc.)

- **WHAT IS IT?** Various plastic products.

- **WHAT CAN IT DO?** Stick like glue to you as well as whatever it was originally on.

- **HOW HARD?** Not easy when fresh; if allowed to dry, you may be stuck with it!

• **WHAT TO DO FIRST:** Get it while it's still wet—don't let it dry. Gently scrape off all you can without spreading it around, and sponge the spot immediately with water to keep the glue gooey.

• **WHAT TO DO NEXT**

Fresh: Although most require a solvent, soap and water will remove some synthetic glues while they're still fresh. Try taking off a little of the glue you probably have on your hands, too, to see if soapy water will do it. If so, go ahead on the fabric. If not, try dry spotter. Acetone may be required to dissolve the clear plastic cements, but don't use acetone on acetate fabrics, and test it first on any fabric! Amyl acetate can be used to remove cements from acetate fabrics, but the acetone in the glue may have already damaged the fabric. Don't use acetone on plastic laminate (Formica) or vinyl. To finish up, use laundry pre-treat on washables and launder as quickly as possible. Take dry cleanables in for dry cleaning.

Old/Dry: If the fabric can stand it, try soaking for half an hour in a boiling solution of vinegar and water (1:10), then launder. Water-rinseable paint and varnish remover will remove some model cements, but test first. Soaking with acetone may do it, too. To be safe, take dry cleanables in for expert spotting.

Hard Surfaces: Dried glue will often chip right off hard surfaces (use your scraper). On porous hard surfaces like brick and concrete, you may need to use one of the spotters suggested under "Fresh" above, but test first to be sure it won't harm the surface.

• **IF THAT DOESN'T DO IT:** Admire it—it'll probably outlast the pyramids!

• **CAUTION:** Don't try to scrape and pick dried glue from fabric—all you're likely to do is damage and distort the fibers or make textured or pile fabrics prematurely bald.

• **PREVENTION:** Use a piece of cardboard or catch cloth behind it next time. Don't put the bottle down anywhere till you put the cap back on. Don't lay the glue tube (or the dripping cap) just anywhere. Don't put on three times more than you need—it doesn't help adhesion, either.

STAIN:
Glue—
Water-Soluble (casein glues such as Elmer's white glue, mucilage, paste, hide glue)

• **WHAT IS IT?** Casein glues, mucilage, and paste are made from milk or from vegetable extracts and starches. Dark wood glues are made from animal by-products such as hides and gelatin, some with petroleum-derived resins.

• **WHAT CAN IT DO?** Leave a hard, raised spot that's not easy to resoften and remove.

• **HOW HARD?** Fairly easy if fresh; certain water-resistant glues can be downright stubborn if allowed to dry (I've even had to **sand** them off).

• **WHAT TO DO FIRST:** Get it while it's still wet—don't let it dry. Gently scrape off all you can without spreading the spot, and immediately sponge with water to keep the glue soft.

• **WHAT TO DO NEXT**
Fresh: Sponge with warm water and soap to remove as much of the glue as possible. If a stain remains, sponge with wet spotter. For animal glues, apply digestant paste, let sit for up to several hours without drying out, then flush with water. Treat washables with laundry pre-treat and wash in warm water.
Old/Dry: If washable, soak in as hot a water bath as the fabric will allow, gently remove as much of the glue as you can after it has softened, then treat as above. If nonwashable fabric, take to dry cleaner for expert spotting.
Hard Surfaces: See Glue—Synthetic.

• **IF THAT DOESN'T DO IT:** Dry cleanables: Take in for expert spotting. Or, if the fabric can stand boiling water, try boiling in a 1:10 solution of vinegar and water for up to 30 minutes, then scrape and rinse.

• **CAUTION:** Don't try to scrape and pick dried glue from fabric—all you're likely to do is damage and distort the fibers or make textured or pile fabrics prematurely bald.

• **PREVENTION:** Use a piece of cardboard or catch cloth behind it next time. Don't put the bottle down anywhere till you put the cap back on. Don't lay the glue tube (or the dripping cap) just anywhere. Don't put on three times more than you need—it doesn't help adhesion, either.

---

grape (see Fruit—Red)

STAIN:
Grass

- **WHAT IS IT?** Tannin, vegetable dye.

- **WHAT CAN IT DO?** Leave a hard-to-remove stain if set by heat or alkali (see Caution below). And make mothers love macadam.

- **HOW HARD?** Manageable if treated when fresh.

- **WHAT TO DO FIRST:** Sponge with plain water.

- **WHAT TO DO NEXT**

    Washables: Sponge with alcohol (test first). If stain remains, soak in digestant for 30 minutes to an hour, rinse thoroughly and launder in warm water with as strong a bleach as is safe for the fabric.

    Dry Cleanables: Sponge with alcohol (test first for colorfastness; dilute alcohol with 2 parts water for acetate fabrics; no alcohol on wool). If stain remains, sponge with vinegar, then with water. If stain remains, apply digestant paste (not on wool or silk), let it sit for 15 to 30 minutes, then sponge with warm water.

IF THAT DOESN'T DO IT: Bleach with hydrogen peroxide.

• **CAUTION:** Don't use alkalis such as ammonia, degreaser, or alkaline detergent—they can set grass stains. Take care in using alcohol—it can make dyes bleed. Spot-bleach dry-cleanable items only as a last resort—the bleached spot may show.

• **PREVENTION:** Do change before you join the touch football game. Don't crouch to admire the chrysanthemums with your good slacks on. Remember that whatever you wear to the company picnic will come back with these.

---

gravy (see Greasy Foods)

STAIN:
Grease

• **WHAT IS IT?** Lubricating or "car" grease (petroleum products); cooking grease (animal fats or vegetable oils), etc.

• **WHAT CAN IT DO?** Leave a semitransparent stain that soon turns dark from all the soil it picks up.

- **HOW HARD?** Fairly simple whether fresh or old.

  WHAT TO DO FIRST: Gently scrape or blot up as much as possible, without forcing it deeper into the surface. Apply an absorbent, and let it stay on as long as needed to soak up as much of the remaining grease as possible.

- **WHAT TO DO NEXT**

  Fresh: Dry Cleanables: Sponge with dry spotter until no more grease is being removed. Washables: Treat with laundry pre-treat, then launder in hot water.

  Old/Dry: Forget the absorbent—it can't do much with dried grease. Rub a little petroleum jelly on the stain, let it sit 15 minutes, then treat as above.

- **IF THAT DOESN'T DO IT:** Dry cleanables: Flush with water and sponge on wet spotter, then flush with water again. Washables: Sponge with dry spotter.

- **PREVENTION:** Put on coveralls or old clothes before fixing **anything** on a car. Don't turn the bacon on high (that's not the right way to make bacon anyway). Don't fill the deep fat fryer too full, and don't sneer at spatter shields. Wear an apron in the kitchen.

STAIN:
Greasy Foods
(butter, margarine, fried foods, mayonnaise, oily salad dressings, gravy, meat juice, etc.)

• **WHAT IS IT?** The All-American stain. Animal fat or vegetable oil, along with dyes and other additives; perhaps protein and starch.

• **WHAT CAN IT DO?** Besides up your cholesterol count, most oily stains of this type oxidize within a matter of days (faster with heat), into a dark, stubborn stain.

• **HOW HARD?** Fairly easy when fresh. If heated or left to oxidize, can be difficult or impossible to remove.

• **WHAT TO DO FIRST:** If there's any solid material on the surface, such as a glob of butter or salad dressing, gently scrape up as much as possible, taking care not to drive it deeper into the fabric. For remaining oily residues, apply an absorbent and leave it on long enough to absorb as much of the oil or grease as possible (this may take several hours).

• **WHAT TO DO NEXT**
Fresh: Remove absorbent. For washables, treat with laundry pre-treat and launder in hot water; air dry. For dry cleanables, sponge with dry spotter until stain is gone.
Old/Dry: For washables, soak gravy, soup, mayonnaise,

and other oily stains containing protein in warm digestant solution for 30 minutes to an hour. Apply laundry pre-treat, then launder in warm water. For dry cleanables, apply a clean cloth pad moistened with dry spotter and a few drops of mineral oil. Keep the pad dampened with spotter and let it soak for 15 minutes, then sponge thoroughly with dry spotter until the stain is gone.

• **IF THAT DOESN'T DO IT:** If the stain remains after laundering washables, don't hot-air dry or iron the object; let the fabric air dry and sponge with dry spotter. If stain remains after using dry spotter on dry cleanables, sponge stain with water, and apply wet spotter and a few drops of ammonia (no ammonia on silk or wool). Sponge the stain with wet spotter several times, then rinse with water. Protein stains like gravy may benefit from a second digestant soak or an application of digestant paste. Any remaining stains will call for the use of a mild bleach, but make sure it's one safe for the fabric.

• **CAUTION:** Don't just whip out a wet cloth when you get an oily stain—water applied too soon can set them. If unsure of the contents of a food spill, read the ingredients list on the label.

• **PREVENTION:** Don't try to drain the fat off hamburger using a fork and no lid. Shroud yourself in napkins when dealing with lobster in drawn butter, corn on the cob, or French dip. And prepare for the worst when you pour the drippings from a roaster to anywhere.

STAIN:
Gum (chewing gum)

• **WHAT IS IT?** Chicle (natural tree gum), sugar, coloring, flavoring.

• **WHAT CAN IT DO?** Stick tenaciously to carpeting, hair, clothing, floors, sidewalks, bedposts, car doors, under tables, anywhere it lands. Then attract dirt to form a dark, ugly spot.

• **HOW HARD?** It's not easy, and it all depends on where, how much, and how long.

• **WHAT TO DO FIRST:** If the gum is soft, remove as much of it as you can by gently pulling it free with your fingers. Freeze what remains with aerosol "gum freeze" (see p. 72), or with dry ice or an ice cube. The gum freeze is by far the most effective of the three. Small objects can just be placed in the freezer.

- **WHAT TO DO NEXT**

Fresh: The moment the spot seems to be frozen stiff, give it a few quick whacks with the handle of a butter knife, while the gum is still cold and brittle. Then rub the dull edge of the knife blade briskly back and forth over the fractured glob. The gum will break up into crumbs and release from the fabric. This works especially well on carpeting, but may be too aggressive an approach for delicate fabrics. For fabrics that can't stand the knife blade rubdown, just break the frozen gum with the knife handle and scrape it free with your fingernail. It's important to pick up or shake off all the little crumbs, or they'll just soften up and redeposit as soon as they warm up. Remove any remaining residue with dry spotter.

Old/Dry: Forget trying to pull any of it off, just go directly to the freeze step and treat as above. If gum is in hair, or somewhere freezing won't work, De-Solv-it or peanut butter will soften it so you can work it loose. The resulting oily spot and remaining gum residue can then be removed with dry spotter (or shampoo, in the case of hair).

Hard Surfaces: On slick hard surfaces like floors, the whole glob can often be popped right off with a putty knife (be careful not to gouge the surface). If it's too gooey, you can freeze first before you pry.

- **IF THAT DOESN'T DO IT:** For washables, apply laundry pre-treat and launder in warm water. For dry cleanables, sponge with dry spotter.

- **CAUTION:** Don't use heat of any kind, and don't iron until you're sure all traces of the stain are gone. Don't handle gum spots outside on a hot day without freezing them first, or you'll spread sticky gum strands all over.

- **PREVENTION:** Put up no-chewing signs ("Ill bred, enough said") or chew out the chewer. Never drop gum on floors or sidewalks or out car windows, or dispose of it anywhere without at least wrapping it in paper. Bare gum is as big a menace as bare steel.

hair coloring (see Dye)
hair oil (see Lotion)

STAIN:
Hard-Water Stains

• **WHAT IS IT?** Minerals (from dissolved rock in the water), which are deposited on windows, bathroom fixtures, and other surfaces when hard water evaporates.

• **WHAT CAN IT DO?** Aside from lowering your housekeeping reputation, it leaves a cloudy and scaly buildup on the surface of things. It can bond permanently to window glass with time and exposure to sunlight.

- **HOW HARD?** Not too bad if treated before it gets too thick. Hard to remove without damaging the surface by the time the buildup is old and heavy. The hardest part of all is ignoring all the bad advice you're offered on how to get rid of it.

- **WHAT TO DO FIRST:** Prevention is the best bet—see below.

- **WHAT TO DO NEXT**
Fresh: Light, newly formed mineral scale can be wiped off hard surfaces with a weak solution of phosphoric acid such as Showers N Stuff. Used regularly, this will keep showers, faucets, and windows free of stains.
Old/Heavy: Old, thick deposits can be tough. For this you want use **straight** Showers N Stuff, or a phosphoric acid cleaner containing at least 9 percent phosphoric acid, available from a janitorial-supply store. Put it on full strength and let it soak for a few minutes. Then scrub with a white nylon scrub pad. Repeat until stain is gone, then rinse with water.

- **IF THAT DOESN'T DO IT:** (And it won't if you or the chemical you apply are weak willed.) Repeat above. For toilet bowls with heavy rings, a strong hydrochloric acid bowl cleaner from a janitorial-supply store can be used, and/or a pumice bar (wet the pumice bar to keep it from scratching).

- **CAUTION:** Resist the urge to use strong chemicals such as hydrochloric acid bowl cleaners on sinks, showers, chrome faucets, etc. It will take the lime scale off faster, but it'll also damage tile grout, metals, plastics, and other surfaces. Sandpaper, chisels, and dynamite are out, too, no matter how tempting.

- **PREVENTION:** Rip out those shower doors (they're nothing but a sliding display area for hard-water scum) and replace them with a nice friendly inexpensive shower curtain you can just toss in the washer. You can also get a water softener, wipe down the shower walls before you step out, apply lemon oil after cleaning to resist buildup, adjust lawn sprinklers away from windows, etc.

STAIN:
Heel Marks on Floors

• **WHAT IS IT?** A smear of black sole material, scuffed off onto the floor as people walk over it.

• **WHAT CAN IT DO?** Make the place look like a drag strip and cause family fights.

• **HOW HARD?** Depends on how many there are, and how tall you are. The marks aren't hard to remove, but if you aren't careful how you go about it you'll leave dull spots on the floor.

• **WHAT TO DO FIRST:** Determine whether the floor has a finish (wax) on it or not—this makes a difference in how you go about things.

• **WHAT TO DO NEXT**

No-Wax Floors: Put a dab of dry spotter on the mark and rub it with a cloth. This should dissolve it. For heavy deposits, scrubbing lightly with a white nylon scrub pad is better and quicker. Use a clean cloth to buff the spot dry and shiny when you're done.

Waxed Floors: Don't use any solvent or harsh cleaners here to soften the mark, because they'll soften and remove the wax, too. Scrub the mark lightly until it's gone with a white nylon scrub pad dipped in neutral detergent solution. A good time to do this is right before you do your regular mopping. If a dull area is left when it dries, buff it out with a soft cloth or apply a dab of floor finish.

• **CAUTION:** Avoid the common impulse to attack these marks with steel wool pads or cleanser. You'll end up with **white** marks and scratches.

• **PREVENTION:** Get rid of shoes that leave black marks, and strike black-soled guests from your list. (Or make them de-shoe at the door.)

---

hide glue (see Glue—Water-Soluble)

STAIN:
Honey, Molasses, Syrup (corn or maple)

- **WHAT IS IT?** Sugar, water, maybe coloring.

- **WHAT CAN IT DO?** Besides attract flies? Leave a sticky raised spot that hardens with age and will set with heat.

- **HOW HARD?** Easy when fresh, only a little more difficult when old and dry, if not heat-set

---

- **WHAT TO DO FIRST:** Gently scrape to remove as much of the syrup as you can from the surface. Soak hardened stains with warm water before scraping. Be careful not to damage the fabric, countertop, or carpet when you're scraping loose that crystallized crud.

- **WHAT TO DO NEXT**
  Washables: Sponge with warm water until all of the sticky residue is gone. Apply laundry pre-treat and wash in warm water. Air dry.
  Dry Cleanables: If the fabric is water-sensitive (delicate silk, rayon, some woolens), send out for expert spotting. If the fabric can tolerate a little water, sponge with warm water until all of the sticky residue is gone. Sponge with wet spotter and a few drops of vinegar. Rinse with water and air dry. If a spot remains, sponge with dry spotter and feather.

• **IF THAT DOESN'T DO IT:** Soak washables in digestant for 30 minutes to an hour and relaunder. Use digestant paste on dry cleanables, let sit for 30 minutes without drying out, then rinse with warm water; feather.

• **CAUTION:** Don't hot-air dry or iron the item, or use hot water on it, until the stain is gone—heat will set sugar stains.

• **PREVENTION:** Remember that syrup bottles always have syrupy sides, and watch where you set that sticky spoon. Don't tuck that little leftover packet of syrup or honey in your pocket or purse as you leave the restaurant unless your memory matches your thrift.

---

hot melt glue (see Glue—Synthetic)

STAIN:
Ice Cream, Milkshakes (all flavors except chocolate; for chocolate ice cream, see Chocolate)

• **WHAT IS IT?** Yummy enough to be worth it. Ice cream contains animal fat, sugar, food color (dye), flavorings, maybe fruit, etc. Many milkshakes—and for that matter some ice

creams—have far more smootheners, thickeners, and emulsifiers than actual dairy products in them.

• **WHAT CAN IT DO?** Some flavors with strong colors can leave permanent stains; sugar and fruit stains will both set hard with heat if not removed.

• **HOW HARD?** Vanilla and light-colored flavors are easy if caught while fresh; raspberry ripple and all its relatives can be more difficult.

• **WHAT TO DO FIRST:** Put that cone down and treat the stain while fresh if possible. Scrape and blot to remove all you can, and sponge with neutral detergent solution or at least with water, no matter where you are.

• **WHAT TO DO NEXT**
   Fresh: Washables: Apply laundry pre-treat and launder in warm water. Air dry. If oily stain remains when dry, sponge with dry spotter. If stain remains from flavoring, soak in digestant for 30 minutes to an hour and relaunder in warm water. Dry

Cleanables: Sponge with wet spotter and a few drops of ammonia (no ammonia on silk or wool). Sponge-rinse with warm water. Air dry. If only stain remains when dry, sponge with dry spotter. If stain remains from flavoring, apply digestant paste (except no digestant on silk or wool), keep moist for 30 minutes, and rinse with warm water.

Old/Dry: After scraping to remove all you can, sponge with dry spotter, then treat as above.

• **IF THAT DOESN'T DO IT:** Treat as a Dye stain.

• **CAUTION:** Don't launder in hot water. Don't dry with heat or iron until stain is completely gone—heat can make sugar and fruit stains permanent.

• **PREVENTION:** Don't try to eat ice cream while driving, and remember that double-dip means double-drip!

STAIN:
Ink—Ballpoint Pen

• **WHAT IS IT?** One of our least favorite stains, for sure! Ballpoint ink is various pigments and dyes in a base of solvents, oils, and resins. There are so many ink recipes around it's impossible to know which one you're dealing with—you just have to experiment a little. Red ink has to be treated differently from all other colors (see below).

- **WHAT CAN IT DO?** Some ballpoint inks can leave a permanent stain—cheap pens are usually the worst.

HOW HARD? With patience and persistence, most ballpoint inks are removable, especially from synthetic fibers. But some inks won't come out, especially from cotton and wool, for anything short of scissors.

- **WHAT TO DO FIRST:** Treat it as soon as possible—it's much easier when fresh. If you can identify the offending pen, put a smudge of ink on a scrap of similar fabric and test to see which of the following procedures works best.

- **WHAT TO DO NEXT**
Washables: Sponge with water. If color transfers to your sponging cloth, keep sponging with water until no more color is coming out. Blot dry. Saturate the stain with cheap hair spray and blot it through into a fresh cloth—continue until no more color is being transferred. Apply laundry pre-treat and launder in warm water; air dry. This will remove most ballpoint ink stains. (Magic Wand laundry stain removal stick works well on some inks, in place of the hair spray and pre-treat.)

Dry Cleanables: For an expensive garment, especially silk, wool, rayon, or acetate, the safest course is to take it in for professional spotting and cleaning. If you're feeling extra brave, or it's a garment you're not deeply attached to, try the procedures for washable garments. When you get to the laundering part, just rinse with warm water and air dry.

- **IF THAT DOESN'T DO IT:** If stain remains after laundering, air dry—don't use heat. Try the following solvents one after the other (pretest first!) until you find one that removes the ink; then sponge the stain with it until no more color comes out: dry spotter, alcohol, acetone (don't use acetone on acetate), amyl acetate. If stain remains, use color remover or a bleach safe for the fabric. If a yellow stain remains, treat as a rust stain.

• **CAUTION:** All of the spotting agents listed in "If That Doesn't Do It," above, can be hazardous—either to you or to what you're working on. Follow all label directions and safety precautions, and don't fail to pretest the fabric in a hidden place.

• *FOR RED INK:* First treat as for red Dye, then go to "If That Doesn't Do It," above, if necessary.

• **PREVENTION:** Beware of pens that have been sticking tip-down in penholders or desktop mugs for longer than anyone can remember. Do clean off pen tips when they get drippy and linty, but resist the impulse to do it with your fingers. Click it—or cap it—before you put it in your pocket.

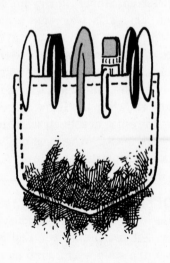

STAIN:
Ink—Felt-tip Markers

- **WHAT IS IT?** Dye and solvents.

- **WHAT CAN IT DO?** Make your cuff, wall, or tablecloth pretty gaudy for a while, or live up to that "permanent" on the label.

- **HOW HARD?** There are two kinds of markers; permanent and nonpermanent ("washable"). Most permanent marker stains will not come completely out (now you know what to use on the marriage license). The nonpermanent type can usually be removed, but some take more work than others.

- **WHAT TO DO FIRST:** Try to identify the culprit marker —it helps a lot to know which type you're dealing with. If the stainee is expensive, or one you hate to lose, take it in for professional spotting. There's no guarantee it'll come out, but the chances are better in the hands of a pro. If you don't know what the marker was, first try the nonpermanent procedure, then the permanent one if a stain remains.

- **WHAT TO DO NEXT**
  Nonpermanent:: For dry-cleanable items, especially expensive garments or delicate fabrics, the best bet is professional spotting and dry cleaning. For washables (or dry cleanables you're willing to take a chance on), try this: Sponge the stain

(being careful not to spread it) with dry blotter. Continue until no more color is being removed. For washables, apply laundry pre-treat, along with a few drops of ammonia, and launder garment in warm water. For carpet, upholstery, and nonwashable fabrics, apply laundry pre-treat and ammonia, tamp, then rinse with warm water.

Permanent:: Don't get your hopes up, but the following procedures will sometimes remove permanent marker stains, and will almost always lighten them somewhat: Sponge the stain repeatedly with ditto fluid, obtainable at an office supply store. If that doesn't do it, try Cutter insect repellent lotion—just rub it in, wait a few minutes, then rinse with water. Pretest these solvents first, and don't use the Cutter on Spandex, rayon, acetate, plastic, vinyl, or paint.

• **IF THAT DOESN'T DO IT:** Sponge with alcohol (test first). If stain remains, bleach with hydrogen peroxide. And remember all this at gift time when you're tempted to buy "a set" for the nephews and nieces.

• **CAUTION:** When you first start on a marker stain, be very careful not to spread it. There's a lot of strong dye there, and it'll go a long way. Use spotter sparingly and blot gently, keeping the wetted area as small as you can.

• **PREVENTION:** Remember that the soft tip of a felt-tip pen can not only stain but keep on drawing out ink, and staining, till the whole marker is empty. So think CAP! before you plunge it into your pocket, purse, or briefcase. Don't lay uncapped markers down anywhere, and remember that markers with square or hexagonal sides are far less likely to roll out of control.

STAIN:
Ink—India

- **WHAT IS IT?** Carbon or "lamp" black in a shellac or gelatin base.

- **WHAT CAN IT DO?** If it dries, you're just about guaranteed a permanent stain.

- **HOW HARD?** Possible to remove from some surfaces if caught immediately. Once it's dry, it rarely can be removed completely.

- **WHAT TO DO FIRST** (After wishing you'd picked a more forgiving medium): **Immediately** flush the fabric with plenty of cool water, until as much pigment as possible has been removed.

- **WHAT TO DO NEXT**
  Fresh: After flushing with water, sponge with ammonia and rinse (dilute ammonia 1:1 with water for silk or wool; if ammonia causes color change in any fabric, apply vinegar and rinse). For washables, then apply laundry pre-treat and launder in warm water. Take dry cleanables in for expert spotting and cleaning.
  Old/Dry: Washables: Soak overnight in a solution of 4 tablespoons ammonia to one quart water, apply laundry pre-treat, and launder in warm water. Dry cleanables: If the piece is valuable, take it in for expert spotting, but don't expect a miracle.

• **IF THAT DOESN'T DO IT:** Forget it. Bleach won't affect carbon stains.

• **PREVENTION:** Keep permanent inks out of the reach of children, and put on old clothes or an apron before using them. Don't plunge your pen or brush in too deep, and refill the bottle before it drops down below half.

---

insecticide (see Chemical Stains, p. 89)

STAIN:
Jam or Jelly, Fruit Syrups

• **WHAT IS IT?** Fruit, sugar.

• **WHAT CAN IT DO?** If you let it go, the sugar will turn yellow with age and heat. There may also be staining from the natural dyes in the fruit.

• **HOW HARD?** Spots from light-colored jams and jellies are easy to remove if not set by heat or soap. Some of the red or purple jelly stains can be perplexing. Then, too, like a wood tick, it depends on whether it's on or **in**.

- **WHAT TO DO FIRST:** Scrape to remove as much as possible, and sponge with warm water.

- **WHAT TO DO NEXT**

Washables: Apply laundry pre-treat, then sponge thoroughly with water to remove sugar residue. If stain remains, treat as for Fruit. If the spot seems to be gone, launder in warm water.

Dry Cleanables: Sponge thoroughly with warm water to remove sugar residue. If stain remains, treat as for Fruit. Don't forget to feather the edges.

Old/Dry: Apply glycerin to soften the stain, let it sit 30 minutes, and rinse with warm water. Treat as above. If the stain has been ironed, it may be permanent.

- **CAUTION:** Don't hot-air dry, or iron the object, or use hot water on it, until the stain is gone—heat will set it. Don't use soap—it will set fruit stains.

- **PREVENTION:** Stop spreading an inch before the edge of the sandwich. Stop pouring as soon as there's a **small** puddle of elderberry syrup around the pancake. Don't serve jelly donuts to anyone under twenty-one.

Jell-O (see Kool-Aid)

jelly (see Jam)

STAIN:
Kool-Aid
(and similar stains from Jell-O, Popsicles, etc.)

- **WHAT IS IT?** Food dye, used to color many cosmetics and medicines as well as foods and beverages. Red dye is the worst offender, with orange following right behind on the "least wanted" list.

- **WHAT CAN IT DO?** Since this is the same type of dye used to color carpet and clothing fabrics, it's no wonder it can leave a permanent stain. The strongly colored food simply re-dyes the fabric. The sugar can leave a stain, too, if not rinsed out.

- **HOW HARD?** One of the worst. Until recently, Kool-Aid stains in non-stain-resistant carpet were often permanent, but products have now been developed to remove them (see below). The new "stain-blocking" carpets are much less susceptible to stains of this type.

• **WHAT TO DO FIRST:** If you can catch a Kool-Aid or food dye spill quickly (within a minute or two), you can neutralize it with a mild ammonia solution (one tablespoon ammonia in a cup of water). On nylon carpeting and some fabrics, this will keep any dye transfer from taking place.

• **WHAT TO DO NEXT**

Fresh: Treat as quickly as possible. Neutralize with ammonia, as above. Rub table salt into the stain and let it sit for a few minutes to absorb the stain. Vacuum out salt and repeat, if necessary. Rinse with water.

Old/Dry: Call in a pro. Professional carpet cleaners now have products specially designed to remove red Kool-Aid and other difficult food dye stains. Be sure the one you consult is familiar with these products, such as Kool Off, Red Out, or Stain Away. They require special training to use and are only available to pro cleaners, but in the hands of a pro they can be a lifesaver. Expert dry cleaners will also have specialized products to remove these stains.

• **IF THAT DOESN'T DO IT:** Treat as for Dye. If that doesn't do it, enlist the help of a professional—dry cleaner for clothing, carpet cleaner for carpeting.

• **PREVENTION:** Serve lemonade instead.

---

lemon (see Fruit—Clear)

lime (see Fruit—Clear)

STAIN:
Lipstick,
Shoe Polish
(paste, not liquid)

• **WHAT IS IT?** Dye in an oil-soluble wax base.

• **WHAT CAN IT DO?** Leave an intensely colored stain that can be easily spread, and tends to set with heat and age.

• **HOW HARD?** Tough even when handled immediately. Can be impossible to completely remove if old and set.

• **WHAT TO DO FIRST:** Gently pluck and scrape to remove as much solid material from the surface as possible. Be careful not to spread the stain or force it in deeper. Don't use any water, wet spotters, or heat at first—these will only spread and set the stain.

• **WHAT TO DO NEXT**
Fresh: Blot with dry spotter. Change your blotting cloth often to carry away dye dissolved by the spotter. Change sponging pad as needed, too, to avoid redepositing dissolved color. Be careful not to spread the stain. Work in vegetable oil, mineral oil, or shortening, let it sit 15 minutes, and sponge again with dry spotter. Sponge remaining dye stain with wet spotter and a few drops of ammonia, tamping if fabric will tolerate it (no ammonia on silk or wool). Apply laundry pre-treat and launder

washables in hot water. Rinse dry cleanables with warm water.

Old/Dry: Apply petroleum jelly and allow to sit 30 minutes to soften stain, then treat as above.

• **IF THAT DOESN'T DO IT:** Sponge with alcohol (test first) and rinse with water. Use chlorine bleach on any remaining stain, if fabric will tolerate it (test first). Professional spotting or color stripping may be required.

• **CAUTION:** A little of this stuff goes a long way, so take extra care to remove as much solid matter as possible before applying solvent. There's a lot of dye in even a tiny particle of these things, and you sure want to remove as much as you can before starting to dissolve it. If it's a valuable piece, the safest bet is to take it in for expert spotting. Ditto if you get a "lipstick load" of stained garments from washing something with a tube of lipstick left in a pocket.

• **PREVENTION:** Stop pretending that you'll ever do a shoe without dropping black or burgundy globs somewhere. Put down those old papers Mother always insisted on and polish your pumps *before* you slip into the white sheath. And as for lipstick, if you really love him (or have to do his laundry), maybe you shouldn't apply a second coat right before he walks in the door.

Liquid Paper (see Correction Fluid)

STAIN:
Liquor (including mixed drinks and white wine; for beer see Beer and for red or rosé wine see Wine)

- **WHAT IS IT?** Water, alcohol; possibly tannin, fruit, sugar, food dyes, and other additives, depending on the type of spirits and mixer.

- **WHAT CAN IT DO?** Alcohol can "burn" woolen fabrics, and it will oxidize and turn brown with age if left to dry on any fabric. It'll also bleed dye from many fabrics, especially acetate.

- **HOW HARD?** Can be difficult if dried, but it's usually no problem if you get it while it's still wet, as long as there's no dye change. Dye changes are permanent.

• **WHAT TO DO FIRST:** Blot up all you can and sponge the spot with cool water.

• **WHAT TO DO NEXT**
Fresh: Work in wet spotter or undiluted neutral detergent along with a few drops of vinegar. Rinse. Launder washables as soon as possible in warm water. Take dry cleanables in for expert spotting if any stain remains.
Old/Dry: For washables, soak the garment in cool water overnight, then treat as above. For dry cleanables, rub in warm glycerin, let it sit for 30 minutes, then treat as above. Take valuable dry cleanables in for expert spotting and cleaning as soon as possible.

• **IF THAT DOESN'T DO IT:** Try digestant (soak for washables, paste for dry cleanables), then launder or rinse with warm water. Some alcohol stains may require treatment with a mild bleach for complete removal.

• **CAUTION:** Don't iron a sugar-based stain or dry with hot air unless you're absolutely sure it's gone—heat can make it permanent. Don't use soap if the drink contains fruit or fruit juice.

• **PREVENTION:** Don't order anything brightly colored or complicated on planes, trains, or riverboat cruises or anyplace you're likely to get up and down a lot. Toast your Blue Hawaiian carefully and don't set the Royal Purple Punch out on your best tablecloth. Bear in mind that every drink after the first one has a better chance of being spilled, slopped, dripped, or dribbled.

STAIN:
Lotion (hand lotion, body lotion, suntan lotion, hair oil)

• **WHAT IS IT?** Mineral or vegetable oil, glycerin, moisturizers, perfume, dye.

• **WHAT CAN IT DO?** Leave an oil slick that attracts dirt—the darkened, dirty areas on the arms and headrest of upholstered chairs are typical.

• **HOW HARD?** Comes off most things easily when fresh; oxidizes and hardens with age.

• **WHAT TO DO FIRST:** For fresh spills or heavy deposits, apply an absorbent and leave on for several hours to blot up the excess oil. Shake or brush off when dry.

• **WHAT TO DO NEXT**
Carpet and Upholstery: Apply dry spotter, tamp, and blot. Continue until the stain is gone. Sponge with neutral detergent solution, rinse, and blot.
Dry Cleanables: Sponge repeatedly with dry spotter until the stain is gone, then feather.
Washables: Apply laundry pre-treat, then smear the spot with petroleum jelly and wash in hot water.
Old/Dry: Apply glycerin or petroleum jelly to soften the stain, then treat as above.

• **IF THAT DOESN'T DO IT:** Sponge with wet spotter and a few drops of ammonia (no ammonia on silk or wool). Rinse with water.

• **PREVENTION:** This stuff is sooo soothing we glom it on double thick and splash it everywhere. Go easy, and give it a chance to be absorbed before you leave the bathroom or lower yourself onto the chaise lounge.

STAIN:
Makeup (liquid foundation makeup, mascara, blusher, eye shadow, etc.)

• **WHAT IS IT?** Dye in various wax and oil-base creams, emulsions, and powders.

• **WHAT CAN IT DO?** Leave a strongly colored stain that's easy to spread.

• **HOW HARD?** Usually removable, but can be as hard as making ourselves look beautiful some days, particularly if set by heat.

• **WHAT TO DO FIRST:** Gently brush or scrape to remove

as much solid material from the surface as possible, being careful not to force the stain deeper in.

• **WHAT TO DO NEXT**

Fresh: Blot with dry spotter and change your blotting pad often to carry away dye dissolved by the spotter. Be careful not to spread the stain. If color remains, apply vegetable oil, mineral oil, or shortening, let it sit 15 minutes, and sponge again with dry spotter. Sponge any remaining dye stain with wet spotter and a few drops of ammonia, tamping if fabric will tolerate it (no ammonia on silk or wool). Change sponging pad, too, as needed to avoid redepositing color. Apply laundry pretreat and launder washables in hot water if safe for the fabric. Rinse dry cleanables with warm water.

Old/Dry: Apply petroleum jelly and allow to sit 30 minutes to soften stain, then treat as above.

• **IF THAT DOESN'T DO IT:** Sponge with alcohol (test first) and rinse with water. Use chlorine bleach on any remaining stain, if fabric will tolerate it (test first). Professional spotting or color stripping may be required.

• **CAUTION:** With potent stainmakers like these take extra care to remove as much of it as possible before applying solvent. There's a lot of dye in this stuff, and you sure want to remove as much as you can before starting to dissolve it. If it's a valuable piece, the safest bet is to take it in for expert spotting.

• **PREVENTION:** Washing your face before bed is kinder to complexions as well as pillowcases. And make sure that bottles and compacts are securely closed before you pop them back into your purse or pocket.

---

maple syrup (see Honey)

margarine (see Greasy Foods)

mascara (see Makeup)

mayonnaise (see Greasy Foods)

meat juice (see Greasy Foods)

meat label stains (see Dye)

Mercurochrome (see Dye)

Merthiolate (see Dye)

STAIN:
Mildew

- **WHAT IS IT?** A tiny live plant—a fungus.

- **WHAT CAN IT DO?** Make the bathroom and a lot of other places mighty unromantic. Mildew leaves black, gray, orange, blue or white specks or splotches on the surface of whatever it's growing on, and it will gradually digest and destroy organic materials like cloth, paper, and wood.

- **HOW HARD?** One of the worst, since it isn't just a stain, it's actually a menace to the material it's on. If your jute-backed carpet gets flooded, mildew can eat away half the strength of the backing in just a few days. And mildew is **alive**, so it can spread and multiply!

- **WHAT TO DO FIRST:** Kill it so it can't do any more damage. Mildew thrives in dark, damp, warm, poorly ventilated conditions. Just putting the object out in the sunlight or drying it out will slow mildew growth dramatically.

- **WHAT TO DO NEXT**
  Hard Surfaces: For bleach-safe surfaces such as tiled tub and shower enclosures and painted walls, use a 1:5 solution of liquid chlorine bleach in cool water. Apply and scrub with a stiff nylon scrub brush, then rinse. This not only kills the mildew, but bleaches out the stains in the grout.
  Garments: Washables: Brush off as much of the mildew specks as you can; wash the garment with chlorine bleach if the

fabric and color can tolerate it. Mildew stains are so sinister, you should consider using bleach even on garments you normally wouldn't. Just be sure to test for colorfastness. Dry cleanables should be taken in immediately for professional cleaning.

Leather (finished leather): Take the mildewed article outside if possible and gently brush all the surface specks away. Then wipe the object all over with a 50/50 solution of isopropyl alcohol and water, and leave it in the sun if possible to get good and dry before you put it back away.

Carpeting: When jute-backed carpeting gets wet (and anything manufactured before 1985 is probably jute), it's important to get it dried out as quickly as possible. Steam cleaning or "extracting" it isn't enough. The carpet needs to be either taken up and dried or dried in place with special fans that balloon the carpet up and blow air underneath. Your local carpet cleaner is the expert who will know how to do all this. Ideally, the back of the carpet should also be treated with a mildewcide.

• **IF THAT DOESN'T DO IT:** You might consider moving to the Sahara.

• **CAUTION:** When working with chlorine bleach, remember not to mix it with any other cleaning compounds except laundry detergent. Combining it with strong acids or alkalis (ammonia, degreaser, lye) can produce deadly gases.

• **PREVENTION:** Don't put **anything** away wet—especially not rolled up or sealed up or wadded up and wet.

STAIN:
Milk (cream)

- **WHAT IS IT?** Animal fat, albumin, water.

- **WHAT CAN IT DO?** Set and get smelly if not removed.

- **HOW HARD?** Simple if caught when fresh. Hard if heat-set.

- **WHAT TO DO FIRST:** Don't wait. Blot up all you can immediately with a dry cloth

---

- **WHAT TO DO NEXT**
  Fresh: Washables: Sponge with cool water. Apply laundry pre-treat and let it sit for a few minutes, then launder in cool water. Air dry. Sponge any remaining stain with dry spotter. If stain remains, soak in digestant for 30 minutes to an hour and relaunder. Dry Cleanables: Sponge with neutral deter-

gent solution and a few drops of ammonia (no ammonia on silk or wool), then with cool water. Let dry, then sponge with dry spotter. If stain remains, apply digestant paste (not on silk or wool), let it sit for 30 minutes without drying out, then rinse. Don't forget to feather edges with each step.

Old/Dry: Scrape to remove residue. Sponge with dry spotter, then treat as above.

• **IF THAT DOESN'T DO IT:** Treat with as strong a bleach as the fabric will tolerate.

• **PREVENTION:** Keep the bucket away from Bossy's back legs, and count on the cat sticking his head in the dish just as you start to pour.

---

milkshakes (see Ice Cream)

mixed drinks (see Liquor)

model cement (see Glue—Synthetic)

molasses (see Honey)

mucilage (see Glue—Water-Soluble)

STAIN:
Mud (dirt)

- **WHAT IS IT?** Soil and water.

- **WHAT CAN IT DO?** Make you look like you just came in from the north forty. And if you scrub it around while it's wet, it'll spread and get embedded.

- **HOW HARD?** Usually easy to remove, except for strongly colored soils.

- **WHAT TO DO FIRST:** Let it dry! Then dry-brush or vacuum away as much of it as possible before wetting the stain. You can get rid of 90 percent of most mud stains this way.

- **WHAT TO DO NEXT**
  Washables: Apply laundry pre-treat and launder in warm water. This will remove all but the toughest mud stains.

Dry Cleanables: Sponge with neutral detergent solution, then rinse with water. If stain remains, sponge with wet spotter and a few drops of vinegar. Rinse, feather, and air dry.

• **IF THAT DOESN'T DO IT:** Deeply colored soils may need additional work. Try sponging with alcohol (dilute 1:1 with water for acetate, pretest for colorfastness on any fabric). If a stain still remains, a soak in digestant for 30 minutes to an hour (use a digestant paste on dry cleanables) may help. Red earth stains will sometimes respond to rust remover (see p. 264).

• **PREVENTION:** Get rid of bare dirt in the dooryard and switch to smooth-soled shoes!

STAIN:
Mustard

• **WHAT IS IT?** Turmeric, a bright yellow spice, is what does the staining.

• **WHAT CAN IT DO?** Put you in a mood that's anything but mellow yellow. If mustard is allowed to set, it can be impossible to remove.

• **HOW HARD?** Not easy when fresh, and extremely difficult when set by heat or alkali (ammonia, etc.).

- **WHAT TO DO FIRST:** Scrape and blot to remove all you can, then treat immediately.

- **WHAT TO DO NEXT**
Fresh: Sponge with dry spotter. Tamp as needed while sponging to loosen the stain. For washables, apply laundry pre-treat and a few drops of vinegar, then wash in cool water. For dry cleanables, sponge with wet spotter and a few drops of vinegar, rinse with cool water.
Old/Dry: Scrape away as much of the dried crust as possible, flexing the fabric to break up embedded residue. Apply glycerin and let it sit for 30 minutes, then treat as above.

- **IF THAT DOESN'T DO IT:** Bleach with hydrogen peroxide. Or simply eat what it's on (it might be more nourishing what you usually put it on).

- **CAUTION:** Don't use ammonia or heat—both will set mustard stains.

- **PREVENTION:** Don't eat hot dogs en route, and remember that the spoon is steadier than the squirter. (And as every street vender knows, wrapping a napkin around your "dog" is the **surest** way to prevent mustard stains.)

STAIN:
Mystery Stain
(stain of unknown origin)

- **WHAT IS IT?** If we knew, it wouldn't be a mystery.

- **WHAT CAN IT DO?** Make you very nervous, especially if it's on something expensive. (Maybe it's contagious.)

- **HOW HARD?** We'll hope it's something easy until we're proven wrong.

- **WHAT TO DO FIRST:** See below. If that doesn't shed any light on it, blot or scrape to remove all you can.

- **WHAT TO DO NEXT**
For unknown stains, we always start with solvent spotter—that's the safe way. So first, sponge with dry spotter. If that

doesn't remove it, try the following chemicals in order, until you find something that softens or loosens the stain. Once you find something that works, stay with it until no more color is coming out. Tamp or scrape to help the spotter work, if the fabric will tolerate it. Go to the next chemical only if a stain remains. When the stain is gone, flush or rinse the spotter out as indicated, and let it air dry.

- **Amyl acetate**—flush with dry spotter

- **Cool water**—blot

- **Wet spotter** with a few drops of **vinegar** (no vinegar on cotton or linen)—rinse with water

- **Wet spotter** with a few drops of **ammonia** (no ammonia on silk or wool)—rinse with water

- **Alcohol** (dilute 1:1 with water for use on acetate; test first on any fabric)—rinse with water

- **Bleach**—the strongest bleach safe for the fabric

- **IF THAT DOESN'T DO IT:** Take it in for professional cleaning (but make sure you confess your own unsuccessful attempts to date).

- **CAUTION:** For an unknown spot on something valuable, taking it in immediately for professional spotting and cleaning is unquestionably the best approach.

- **PREVENTION:** If you treat it as soon as it happens, while you still remember what it is, you're much less likely to have mystery stains.

Six Clues for Stain Detectives

If you know what a stain is when you start working on it, the chances of removal are about doubled. What do you do when you run into a mystery stain?

1. **Color** is a real clue. Just remember that as things dry they often change color. Fresh sugar stains are usually light-colored, but old, caramelized sugar is yellow-brown. Brightly colored stains like blood and tomato turn duller and darker as they set. Fruit, grass, ink, and Kool-Aid don't change much in color as they dry. Paint, glue, and nail polish hardly change at all.

2. The **look and feel** of a stain will often give a clue. Is it oily or dry? Opaque or transparent? Built-up and crusty or with no solid material at all showing on its surface? Is it brittle or sticky? Hard or soft? Shiny or dull? Is it all one color or texture or does it seem to be a mix? Thinking about how something looks and feels when it dries will often help solve your mystery. Dried mustard and dried honey can look pretty similar, but the honey will feel stiff, the mustard much softer.

3. It's a safe guess that **sticky, gooey stains are sugar-based:** syrup, molasses, honey, caramelized sugar, soft drinks, etc. Most dried sugar stains will turn white when scratched.

4. Is it an **oil stain?** A lot of stains are oily, and oily stains go dark. A grease stain set by laundering is usually dark brown. Oily stains look a lot alike after they've picked up soil. It may have started out as mayonnaise, margarine, or motor oil, but they all look pretty much the same after they've been walked on awhile. If a dried stain is still soft

Six Clues for Stain Detectives (cont.)

and flexible, is dark and dirty in color, and is soaked into the surface rather than raised, it's likely a grease or oil stain.

5. Liquor, beer, perfume, and many food stains can be identified by their **smell**—so scratch and sniff! Some brave souls with all their inoculations caught up even employ the taste test.

6. **Circumstantial evidence** can also help you pin it down. How big is the spot? Where is it on the chair or cardigan? Is it a single drop or a dribble or a spray? Might there be an imprint along with the stain, to help reveal what you rubbed or leaned against? What **room** is the injured object in, and what kinds of activities take place there? Where was the stained piece last, and what was served or used there? The marks on your college son's clothes might mystify you, for example, till you learn that he recently won the All-Kansas Cow-pie Throwing Contest.

STAIN:
Nail Polish

- **WHAT IS IT?** A very fast-drying enamel or lacquer.

- **WHAT CAN IT DO?** Bond to fibers as it hardens, leaving a stiff raised spot. And the dyes in nail polish can cause permanent stains.

- **HOW HARD?** One of the worst, even if you go after it right away.

- **WHAT TO DO FIRST:** Act fast—nail polishes are designed to dry almost instantly! Blot or gently scrape as much as possible out of the fabric, then immediately apply the proper solvent (see below) to keep the spot from drying out

- **WHAT TO DO NEXT**
Fresh: For acetate, triacetate, modacrylic, rayon, silk, and wool, apply glycerin and take the garment to a dry cleaner

immediately for professional spotting. For other fabrics, dab acetone on an inconspicuous place to test for colorfastness. If you don't have acetone, use a nonoily fingernail polish remover. If color doesn't change, and there's no fabric damage, flush the stain repeatedly with acetone (or polish remover) until no more color is being removed. Tamp as necessary to help loosen the stain. Flush with dry spotter. Air dry. If acetone damages the dye or fabric, use amyl acetate instead.

Old/Dry: Soak the stain with amyl acetate to soften it, then treat as above.

• **IF THAT DOESN'T DO IT:** Sponge with alcohol (test first). Bleach with as strong bleach as the fabric will tolerate. Try color remover as a last resort.

• **CAUTION:** When using acetone, be sure to pretest first, and protect your work area—acetone will soften paint, varnish, and plastics. You don't want to get the stain out and ruin your tabletop in the process. Keep acetone away from sparks or flame, and use only in a well-ventilated area. Don't use acetone on acetate, triacetate, or modacrylic fabrics.

• **IF THAT DOESN'T DO IT:** Snip off the Polynesian Pink part and throw the rest in the rag bag.

• **PREVENTION:** Don't set the polish bottle—even for a second—on the couch arm, the carpet, or the back of the wicker elephant. Don't balance the bottle between your knees or on top of your thigh. Instead make it a habit to put it on a firm flat surface covered with a disposable cloth.

---

newspaper ink (see Carbon Paper)

STAIN:
Oil (automotive, cooking, lubricating)

• **WHAT IS IT?** Vegetable, animal, or petroleum (mineral) oil.

• **WHAT CAN IT DO?** Make the Arabs richer if we spill enough of it. Also leaves a dark penetrating stain that attracts other soil and dirt.

• **HOW HARD?** Fairly simple if not allowed to set and as long as you're not an oil tanker captain.

• **WHAT TO DO FIRST:** Gently scrape or blot up as much as possible, without forcing the stain deeper into the fabric. For fresh stains, apply an absorbent, and let it stay on long enough to soak up as much of the oil as possible.

• **WHAT TO DO NEXT**
Fresh: Dry cleanables: Sponge with dry spotter until no more oil is being removed; feather. Washables: treat with laundry pre-treat, then launder in as hot a water as the fabric will stand.

Old/Dry: Forget the absorbent—it probably won't pick up old, dried oil. Rub a little petroleum jelly on the stain, let it sit 15 minutes, then treat as above.

• **IF THAT DOESN'T DO IT:** Dry cleanables: Flush with water and sponge on wet spotter, then rinse with water. Washables: Sponge with dry spotter.

• **PREVENTION:** If you're man or woman enough to change the oil in your car, you can be careful where you plant your jeans when you come in the house.

orange (see Fruit—Clear)

STAIN:
Oven Cleaner

• **WHAT IS IT?** Usually lye.

• **WHAT CAN IT DO?** Not only eat your skin, but rapidly damage silk and wool, and leave white spots on colored fabrics. It can also injure some paints and varnishes.

• **HOW HARD?** Easy if you get it off fast before any damage has occurred. If not, forget it!

• **WHAT TO DO FIRST:** Act quickly, especially if spilled on silk, wool, skin, or paint. Scrape to remove all you can and immediately flush with cool water.

• **WHAT TO DO NEXT**

Fresh: Sponge with vinegar, then rinse with cool water.

Old/Dry: Soak with mild vinegar solution for a few minutes to neutralize, and rinse with cool water. Then treat as for Fresh. If damage has been done, it can't be reversed.

• **IF THAT DOESN'T DO IT:** Launder washables in warm water; take dry cleanables in for expert cleaning.

• **CAUTION:** Always wear rubber gloves and long sleeves when working with oven cleaner—even if all you're doing is removing it from something. And be careful what you do with this corrosive stuff after you scrape it up!

• **PREVENTION:** Don't wear anything you like a lot when working with oven cleaner. Protect the surroundings well with old papers before you start, or use a brush or cloth to apply this caustic stuff to tricky spots like the door frame and the edges of the door. No one can aim an aerosol well enough to avoid hitting at least two innocent bystanding surfaces.

STAIN:
Paint—Oil-Base

- **WHAT IS IT?** Pigments, alkyd resins, solvents, oil.

- **WHAT CAN IT DO?** Get on anything you don't want it to, always in contrasting color. Then it dries to a hard raised spot that bonds tightly to the fabric and can be impossible to remove.

- **HOW HARD?** A hassle even when wet, depending on the pigments; very difficult when dry.

- **WHAT TO DO FIRST:** Don't let it dry! Blot out as much of the paint as possible with a paper towel or cloth.

- **WHAT TO DO NEXT**
  Fresh: Flush with the solvent called for on the paint container (turpentine or paint thinner for most oil-based paints). Tamp if needed to loosen the spot. If a volatile solvent such as

lacquer thinner or acetone is called for, test before using to prevent fabric damage. If you can't flush solvent through the fabric (upholstered furniture, carpeting, etc.), apply it repeatedly and blot it back out each time until all paint color is removed. Sponge with dry spotter and feather.

Old/Dry: Apply water-rinseable paint and varnish remover and let the spot soften (be sure to test first). Gently scrape away softened paint, and use more paint remover as needed. Tamp as needed to loosen stain. Rinse with water. If paint remains, smear with glycerin and let soak for several hours. Then treat as for Fresh stain.

Hard Surfaces: The easiest solution is to wipe up spatters while they're still wet. Dried specks can be removed from glass and ceramic tile with a razor scraper (be sure to wet the surface first); from aluminum trim and other metals with lacquer thinner. Be careful about using lacquer thinner on such things as Formica, enameled appliances, and vinyl flooring—it can soften the finish if it sits too long. For surfaces that won't stand lacquer thinner or razor scraping, wet with either paint thinner (for oil-base paint) or water (for latex) and scrape gently with a plastic or nylon scraper. Specks on your watch, glasses, and other such delicates are best removed with that exquisitely tuned instrument, the human fingernail. It's hard enough to really work, yet soft enough to not scratch most surfaces, and it's controlled by the world's most sensitive computer. Wetting the surface with the appropriate solvent before any scraping not only lubricates the surface to help prevent scratches, but also softens the paint and makes removal easier.

• **IF THAT DOESN'T DO IT:** Washables: Apply laundry pre-treat and launder in warm water—air dry. Dry cleanables: Apply laundry pre-treat and sponge with cool water—if stain remains, take in for expert spotting. On carpet: You can use needlenose pliers to pinch and pulverize thoroughly dry drops, then vacuum them right up.

• **CAUTION:** The safest course for a dried-out paint stain on an expensive object is to take it in for expert spotting. For everyday things, you might feel brave enough to try the Old/Dry procedure.

• **PREVENTION:** Don't dip your brush up to the knuckles, and try to find a safe place to sit the lid. Or have your not-so-exacting husband take you out of town for the weekend while a professional painter does the whole thing.

STAIN:
Paint—Water-Base
(Latex)

• **WHAT IS IT?** Water, polymer resins, pigments.

• **WHAT CAN IT DO?** Dry to a tough, raised, highly visible spot.

• **HOW HARD?** Fairly easy when fresh because latex paint dissolves in water; can be difficult once it starts to dry. Cures harder and harder over a period of days. Some water-base paints, especially acrylics, are impossible to remove once they've dried.

• **WHAT TO DO FIRST:** Gently blot up all you can with a paper towel, being careful not to drive the paint deeper into the surface. Wet the stain with water immediately thereafter to prevent it from drying out.

- **WHAT TO DO NEXT**
  Fresh: Sponge with warm neutral detergent solution, continuing until no more paint is being removed. For washables, apply laundry pre-treat and launder immediately in warm water, then air dry. For dry cleanables and carpeting, sponge with wet spotter, tamping as needed to loosen any partially dry areas, flush with water, then air dry. For large spills of paint on carpeting, flood the area with water and blot out with towels or a wet/dry vacuum. Continue until no more paint is being removed, then treat as above.
  Old/Dry: Apply water-rinseable paint-and-varnish remover (be sure to test first). This should turn most paint spots to mush. Gently scrape away the paint as it softens, and use more paint remover as needed. Tamp as needed to loosen solids. If paint remains, smear with glycerin and let soak for several hours. Then treat as for Fresh stain.
  Hard Surfaces: See Paint—Oil-Base.

- **IF THAT DOESN'T DO IT:** Sponge with dry spotter and feather.

- **CAUTION:** If you have a dried-out paint stain on an expensive object, the safest course is to take it in for expert spotting. For everyday things, you might feel brave enough to try the Old/Dry procedure.

- **PREVENTION:** Wipe surrounding woodwork/floor/whatever with a damp cloth as soon as you finish painting an area, to catch specks and spatters while they're still wet and easy to remove.

---

paste (see Glue—Water-soluble)
peanut butter (see Greasy Foods)
pear (see Fruit—Clear)

STAIN:
Pencil Lead,
Indelible Pencil

- **WHAT IS IT?** Graphite.

- **WHAT CAN IT DO?** Give you black marks, and leave a streak of imbedded graphite particles.

- **HOW HARD?** Fairly easy on synthetics; can be tricky on white cotton or linen; not a problem on most hard surfaces.

- **WHAT TO DO FIRST:** Vacuum or shake out any loose particles.

- **WHAT TO DO NEXT**
Washables: Use a soft, kneadable art gum eraser to gently blot and wipe out the mark. A soft pencil eraser works, too, but not as well. Be careful not to distort the fabric. Rub in laundry pre-treat, along with a few drops of ammonia, and launder immediately in warm water.

Dry Cleanables: Erase stain as above. Sponge with dry spotter. If stain remains, sponge with wet spotter and a few drops of ammonia. Rinse with warm water and feather.

Hard Surfaces: Pencil will wipe off nonporous surfaces like enamel paint and Formica with a neutral detergent solution. For porous surfaces like raw wood, wallpaper, and flat latex paint, erase with an art gum eraser as above.

• **IF THAT DOESN'T DO IT:** Repeat above. For indelible pencil, sponge with alcohol (test for colorfastness; dilute with two parts water for use on acetate; do not use alcohol on silk or wool).

• **PREVENTION:** Empty the pencil sharpener before it's fall-out-all-over full, and remember to retract the lead in your mechanical pencil before you jam it into your shirt pocket.

STAIN:
Perfume, Cologne

• **WHAT IS IT?** Alcohol, essential oils, fragrances.

• **WHAT CAN IT DO?** Like any alcohol stain, perfume can burn wool, and will eventually oxidize and turn brown on any fabric. The alcohol in perfume or cologne can also cause dye to bleed in some fabrics.

- **HOW HARD?** Not usually a problem if treated when fresh. If left to dry or if dye bleeds, it can be impossible.

- **WHAT TO DO FIRST:** Treat immediately, while still wet. Blot up all you can and sponge the spot with cool water.

- **WHAT TO DO NEXT**

Washables: Apply laundry pre-treat and wash in warm water. If stain remains after laundering, treat as for dry cleanables.

Dry Cleanables: Blot out as much of the water as you can and apply warm glycerin; tamp if the fabric will allow it. Rinse with cool water. If any stain remains, sponge with mild vinegar solution, then rinse with cool water. Blot as dry as possible and feather the edges.

Old/Dry: Take in for expert spotting and cleaning.

- **IF THAT DOESN'T DO IT:** Sponge with alcohol (test first for colorfastness; dilute with two parts water for use on acetate; don't use alcohol on silk or wool).

• **PREVENTION:** Don't squirt the silk blouse or sequined gown front dead center, even if the movie heroines always did. You may end up with a stain in the worst imaginable location. Go for the pulse points like wrists and behind the ears and knees, where perfume has the most powerful effect anyway. And get rid of those dark, rancid, antique colognes littering the cabinet—they're the worst offenders.

STAIN:
Perspiration

• **WHAT IS IT?** Body oils, mineral salts, enzymes.

• **WHAT CAN IT DO?** Not only make you unpopular, but weaken and discolor fabric if not removed.

• **HOW HARD?** Usually no sweat, unless heat-set. Some antiperspirants combine with sweat to make the stain more tenacious.

• **WHAT TO DO NEXT**
Washables: Soak for 30 minutes to an hour in digestant, then launder in warm water. If stain has discolored fabric, use as strong a bleach as is safe for the fabric.
Dry Cleanables: Sponge with dry spotter, then with wet spotter and a few drops of ammonia (no ammonia on silk or wool). Flush with water and feather.

• **IF STAIN OR ODOR REMAINS:** Soak washables in warm salt water (three to four tablespoons per gallon of water), then relaunder.

• **CAUTION:** Never iron anything with untreated perspiration stains—the heat will set them.

• **PREVENTION:** Aside from switching to isometrics, you could wear absorbent underwear such as cotton rather than synthetics to at least help prevent. And if sweat stains are a real problem for you, or you have a truly elegant garment you want to protect, there are such things as underarm shields. (Be careful which brightly colored tops you wear under white jackets—or you'll have a dye stain blended with the sweat stains.)

STAIN:
Pet Stains (urine and feces)

Since pet stains in carpeting are the big problem, the following concentrates on carpet. For pet (and human) waste stains on upholstery and bedding, use the same process, but see p. 143-148 to adapt it to those surfaces.

• **WHAT IS IT?** Protein, urea, organic waste, zillions of bacteria.

• **WHAT CAN IT DO?** They may be more vile-smelling and repelling, but feces are easier to remove and much less of a

threat than urine. If urine penetrates down into the carpet backing and pad and isn't completely removed while fresh, you're in trouble. Urine changes chemically as it dries and ages, and you can end up with permanent yellow stains and a very persistent residual odor.

• **HOW HARD?** If you handle them right away, pet stains can be removed completely. Put off or ignored, they become extremely difficult to impossible. Plus they'll encourage Fido or Feline to encore right in the same place!

• **WHAT TO DO FIRST:** Scrape up any solid matter, being careful not to force it deeper into the pile. Blot up any free liquid by putting a folded towel or absorbent pad over the spot (resist the urge to use Fluffy himself) and pressing gently with your foot. Go easy at first to keep from forcing urine deeper into the carpet. Keep changing the towel and applying increased foot pressure until no more moisture is being transferred to the towel. Finish up by putting your whole weight on the towel, to sop up every last bit of liquid possible.

• **WHAT TO DO NEXT**
Fresh: After scraping and blotting thoroughly, apply Outright Pet Odor Eliminator. It's a bacteria/enzyme digester (see p. 63), the most effective product available for dealing with organic stains and odors. Be sure to follow label directions. Mix only as much as you need for the stain at hand. Don't put any other cleaning agents or spotters on the stain—they'll kill the

digester. For feces stains that didn't penetrate the carpet pile, just sponge with the Outright solution after scraping and cover with a plastic bag to keep the stain wet while the digester works (6 to 8 hours).

For urine or loose, watery feces, apply half again as much Outright solution as you estimate there was urine, so it will soak down as far as the urine did. Put a plastic bag over the stain, and use your foot to push the Outright down into the carpet and pad. Step on it several times, until the area feels thoroughly squishy. Leave the plastic bag in place to keep the spot from drying out, and let it sit for 10 to 12 hours. It takes that much time for the enzymes in the solution to eat all the organic waste. Done properly, this process totally eliminates the urine or feces in the carpet, no matter how deeply imbedded, and prevents any residual odor. If a slight yellow stain remains after the Outright dries, use wet spotter to remove it.

Old/Dry: If you have carpeting riddled with old, dried urine stains that smell bad even after steam cleaning, call in an odor control specialist. The cure will probably involve removing the carpet, sealing the floor, replacing the pad, cleaning and deodorizing the carpet both front and back, and reinstalling it.

• **IF THAT DOESN'T DO IT:** Replace the carpet, put a potted palm over the spot, or consider switching to hermit crabs.

• **CAUTION:** Don't believe the advertising for miracle pet stain removers that "You just spray on and wipe off and the stain disappears like magic!" Anything that works permanently has to get down to the source of the odor and eliminate it. Urine odors treated with quick fixes will be back to haunt you!

Never use ammonia on pet accident sites—its urinelike odor will actually *attract* pets.

• **PREVENTION:** Don't **create** a pet that's accident-prone—

spend the little bit of time it takes to make sure that new puppy is 100 percent housebroken (it'll save lots of cleaning and cussing later). Don't let the litter box get so gross that no self-respecting cat would use it, and don't load your pet up on people food.

---

plant food (see Chemical Stains, p. 89)

polyurethane (see Paint—Oil-Base)

Popsicles (see Kool-Aid)

potato chips (see Fast Food Stains and Greasy Foods)

printer ribbon (see Carbon Paper)

raspberry (see Fruit—Red)

STAIN:
Rust

• **WHAT IS IT?** Iron oxide. Rust stains get on fabrics and other surfaces from contact with wet iron or steel. Those little brown spots on your clothing are probably rust, either from a worn washer or dryer drum or from iron in your water supply. Chlorine bleach causes dissolved iron to precipitate out of water, causing rust stains in the wash. A rust-colored stain on plumbing fixtures is caused by iron in the water, too.

• **WHAT CAN IT DO?** Leave a reddish-brown spot that bonds tightly to the surface.

• **HOW HARD?** Comes off like magic from fabrics treatable with professional rust remover; can be very difficult on delicate fabrics that must be dry cleaned.

• **WHAT TO DO NEXT**

Washables: Unless your son-in-law owns a dry cleaner, the quickest and easiest treatment is with a professional rust remover—just apply it to the stain, and watch it disappear. Professional rust remover is available in janitorial-supply stores under several different brand names, or in variety stores as Whink Rust Stain Remover. Because most of these spotters contain hydrofluoric acid, they're **extremely dangerous** and must be handled very carefully. Don't use on fabrics containing glass or metallic fibers. Be **very careful** not to get any on your skin—it will cause serious burns. Don't get it on glass, porcelain, or enamel surfaces (like the top of your washer) either—it will do damage. And be sure to rinse it out of all fabrics thoroughly with water afterward, for the same reason.

If all this seems a little hairy to you, a fairly reliable home remedy is to apply salt to the stain, then drip on lemon juice. Hold it over steam or let it dry in the sun, then rinse. Repeat as necessary. A lot slower and not nearly as effective as a hydrofluoric rust remover, but safer.

Delicate Fabrics (Silk, wool, fiberglass, metallic fabrics, acetate, rayon): These fabrics can't handle professional rust removers. Take them in for expert spotting. For washable wool garments and wool carpeting, use hot oxalic acid solution (one tablespoon of crystals to one cup of hot water). Apply the solution, then rinse quickly with hot water. Repeat until the stain is gone.

Bathroom Fixtures: For rust stains in sinks and tubs, wet the surface and sprinkle on oxalic acid crystals and let the resulting paste sit until it dries. Rewet, scrub with a white nylon scrub pad, and rinse with water. This also works on concrete, brick, and stone. A pumice bar (available at janitorial-supply stores as Pumie and other brands) can be used for rust stains inside white toilet bowls, but be sure to keep the area wet while you're scrubbing.

• **CAUTION:** Don't use chlorine bleach—it'll only make rust stains worse.

• **PREVENTION:** If you have iron-rich water, leave chlorine bleach out of the laundry. Get rid of that old clothes dryer with the rusty drum.

---

salad dressing (see Greasy Foods)

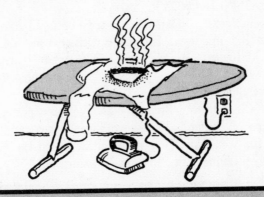

STAIN:
Scorch

• **WHAT IS IT?** A burn, usually from a hot iron. If it's dark, it's probably burned fiber. If it's light, this could be your lucky day; maybe it's only burned starch or soap residue, which will wash out.

- **WHAT CAN IT DO?** Leave a mark on the fabric, ranging from faint tan to dark brown, as well as damage it.

- **HOW HARD?** Light scorch can usually be removed or lightened considerably. Dark scorch is probably permanent—it's particularly difficult to remove from silk and wool.

- **WHAT TO DO FIRST:** Be aware of the fact that if the fibers are significantly scorched, they'll be weakened, and anything you do may cause further damage (but then what have you got to lose?).

- **WHAT TO DO NEXT**
  Washables: Rub laundry pre-treat or liquid-detergent into the stain and launder in hot water with chlorine bleach, if the fabric will tolerate it. If fabric won't stand chlorine bleach, sponge with hydrogen peroxide and a few drops of ammonia before washing.
  Dry Cleanables: Sponge with hydrogen peroxide and a few drops of ammonia. Rinse with cool water and blot dry; feather the wet edge. If a stain remains, you can try professional dry cleaning, but don't expect a miracle.

- **IF THAT DOESN'T DO IT:** Scrubbing the stain lightly with steel wool and then retreating as above will often lighten a bad scorch mark, but it'll probably make the fibers fuzz up.

- **CAUTION:** Don't get your hopes up too high—disappointment is bad for your blood pressure.

- **PREVENTION:** Iron the delicate stuff first, not last, and don't press your luck trying to undo stubborn creases. Don't overdo the spray starch, and don't daydream while ironing!

STAIN:
Shoe Polish
(liquid, including white.
For paste polish, see p. 228-229)

- **WHAT IS IT?** An opaque liquid coating much like shellac.

- **WHAT CAN IT DO?** Dry to a tough coating that bonds very lightly to fibers.

- **HOW HARD?** Difficult even when fresh. The older it gets, the harder it's going to be.

- **WHAT TO DO FIRST:** Treat immediately if possible. Blot up all you can, then follow with dry spotter pronto to keep it from drying out.

- **WHAT TO DO NEXT**

Fresh: Blot with dry spotter. If it dissolves the stain, keep blotting as long as color is coming out. If dry spotter doesn't do it, sponge with alcohol (test first). If stain still remains, apply vegetable oil, mineral oil, or shortening, let it sit 15 minutes, and sponge again with dry spotter. If stain is still there, sponge with amyl acetate until no more color is being removed, then flush with dry spotter and feather.

If all else fails, try dampening the spot with water, adding a few drops of vinegar, and tamping if the fabric will tolerate it. Rinse with water, then continue water, vinegar, and tamping until no more color is coming out.

Old/Dry: Flex the fabric to break up the hardened film, and gently scrape away as much of it as possible. Be careful not to damage the fabric. Treat as above.

• **IF THAT DOESN'T DO IT:** Professional spotting may be required.

• **CAUTION:** This can be a tough one. Don't use too much of any kind of solvent, and take extra care to keep the spot confined to a small area. For valuable garments or furnishings, the safest course is expert spotting and cleaning.

• **PREVENTION:** Question your sanity for wearing white shoes unless your boss makes you wear them. And don't head off to the hospital until they're dry!

shortening (see Greasy Foods)

STAIN:
Smoke/Soot
(except tobacco smoke, for which see p. 227-228)

• **WHAT IS IT?** Tiny particles of oil and carbon that float in the air and land everywhere.

- **WHAT CAN IT DO?** Leave a black oily stain that's easy to spread, and a strong, long-lasting odor. You think you got rid of it six months ago, then it reappears with humid weather.

- **HOW HARD?** Can be difficult indeed on porous absorbent materials such as carpeting, drapes, furniture, and unsealed rock, brick, and wood.

- **WHAT TO DO FIRST:** As soon as you can see, decide whether it's something you really want to handle yourself. If it's a house fire, furnace blowup, or other major or minor calamity, your homeowner's policy probably covers it, and your best bet is to let a smoke damage restoration contractor take care of it. If it's just a light smoke film from a woodstove, overcrisp apple crisp, or a stained fireplace front, or if you're determined to clean up your own disaster, start by removing the residue. Vacuum up any soot or ashes. Remove smoke film from hard surfaces with rubber dry sponges, available at a janitorial-supply store.

- **WHAT TO DO NEXT**
  Clothing: Mist washable clothing with laundry pre-treat (spray heavier on any visible smoke or soot stains), then launder in hot water, with bleach if safe for the fabric. Adding one-half

cup washing soda to the load will help cut the oily deposit. If stains remain, sponge with alcohol. Dry cleanables should be taken in for professional cleaning.

Carpet and Upholstery: Upholstered furniture can be shampooed with carpet and upholstery shampoo (if wet cleaning is safe for the fabric), to which you've added water-soluble deodorizer, available at a janitorial-supply store. If furniture isn't water-safe, sponge it with dry spotter all over, or have it professionally dry-cleaned. NOTE: The odor will still linger in the padding and inaccessible parts of the piece. Airing out will help, but the only real cure is professional deodorizing (fogging with a smoke odor counteractant). Have carpeting professionally steam-cleaned, and ask the technician to add deodorizer to the cleaning solution.

Fireplaces: Scrub stone or brick with a stiff brush and a solution of one-half cup of powdered cold-water laundry detergent per gallon of hot water. Apply plenty so it can float the smoke particles out, and then rinse. If your fireplace is really sooty, it may take several rounds. Apply clear masonry seal after it's all good and dry to prevent further staining.

Walls and Ceilings: Remove smoke film with dry sponges, then wash with a solution of heavy-duty cleaner/degreaser from a janitorial-supply store. Polish dry with a cotton terry cleaning cloth.

• **IF THAT DOESN'T DO IT:** Repainting, refinishing, or replacement will be required.

• **PREVENTION:** Open the chimney damper before you open the stove door and before building a fire in the fireplace. Don't leave the pot roast browning while you go to answer the door—it may take longer than you think.

STAIN:
Soft Drinks

- **WHAT IS IT?** Sugar, coloring, flavorings; tannin in colas and root beer.

- **WHAT CAN IT DO?** Like any sugar spot, can become a permanent yellow stain if heat-set. The tannin and caramel colorings in dark-colored drinks can also stain.

- **HOW HARD?** Easy when fresh, difficult if set.

- **WHAT TO DO FIRST:** Take the time to rinse out the spill when it happens, even if it makes you late getting back from lunch.

- **WHAT TO DO NEXT**
  Fresh: Blot out as much as possible with a clean cloth. Sponge the stain several times with warm (not hot) water. Make sure you get all the sugar out. Then launder washables; feather the spot in dry cleanables and let it air dry.
  Old/Dry: Washables: Soak in digestant for 30 minutes to an hour and launder in warm water. Dry cleanables: Apply glycerin and leave for 30 minutes, then flush with warm water and feather.

- **IF THAT DOESN'T DO IT:** Let fabric dry; sponge with dry spotter, followed by wet spotter and a few drops of vingear. Flush with warm water, blot dry, and feather.

- **CAUTION:** Don't iron or dry with heat until the sugar is completely removed.

- **PREVENTION:** Are you **sure** you want the super maxima size, specially while driving? If you set it on the car floor—anywhere—it'll fall over, and if you tuck it between the seat and door you'll forget it.

STAIN:
Soup

- **WHAT IS IT?** Meat juice, meat, vegetables, oils, maybe milk or cream, sugar. (For tomato soup see Tomato.)

- **WHAT CAN IT DO?** Meat soups leave greasy stains that set with age; strongly colored soups such as borscht can leave vegetable dye stains.

- **HOW HARD?** Duck soup if you do it right away; left to set, can be difficult—particularly meat soups. Because of the combination of ingredients, soup stains often call for a multi-pronged attack.

- **WHAT TO DO FIRST:** Treat immediately by blotting up all you can with a dry cloth.

• **WHAT TO DO NEXT**

Fresh: Washables: Sponge with warm water. Apply laundry pre-treat and let it sit for a few minutes, then launder in warm water. Air dry. Sponge any remaining stain with dry spotter. If stain remains, soak in digestant for 30 minutes to an hour and relaunder. Dry Cleanables: Sponge with neutral detergent solution and a few drops of ammonia (no ammonia on silk or wool), then with cool water. Let dry, then sponge with dry spotter. If stain remains, apply digestant paste (not on silk or wool), let it sit for 30 minutes without drying out, then rinse with water and feather.

Old/Dry: Scrape to remove residue. Sponge with dry spotter, then treat as above.

• **PREVENTION:** When you're deciding on a style of serving, remember that "ladle out" is almost synonymous with "spill." And it's not only good manners to lean forward when you sip, it's smart stain prevention.

STAIN:
Soy Sauce, Worcestershire Sauce

- **WHAT IS IT?** Soy protein, salt, sugar, vinegar, coloring.

- **WHAT CAN IT DO?** Ruin good rice and clothes, nice.

- **HOW HARD?** Difficult even when fresh; can be permanent if set by age or heat.

WHAT TO DO FIRST: Act **immediately**, if possible. Blot up all you can and sponge the spot with cool water.

• **WHAT TO DO NEXT**

Washables: Sponge with mild vinegar solution. Apply laundry pre-treat and wash in cool water. If stain remains, soak in digestant for 30 minutes to an hour and relaunder.

Dry Cleanables: Sponge with wet spotter and a few drops of vinegar, then rinse. If stain remains, apply digestant paste (not on silk or wool), leave it on for 30 minutes without letting it dry, then rinse and feather.

Old/Dry: Smear on glycerin and let it sit for 30 minutes to soften the stain, then treat as above.

• **IF THAT DOESN'T DO IT:** Take valuable pieces in for expert spotting. If it's something you don't mind being a little daring with, sponge it with alcohol (test for colorfastness first, dilute alcohol 1:1 with water for acetate or wool). Rinse.

• **CAUTION:** Don't use heat until you're sure it's gone.

• **PREVENTION:** Don't trust that shaker nozzle to stay in place, and beware of sauces in slippery, drippy plastic envelopes.

---

spaghetti sauce, red (see Catsup)

steak sauce (see Catsup)

stickers (see Adhesives)

suntan lotion (see Lotion)

Super Glue (see Glue—Synthetic)

tape (see Adhesives)

STAIN:
Tar

- **WHAT IS IT?** Asphalt waterproofing material, used on roofs, for paving, street patching, etc.

- **WHAT CAN IT DO?** Find its way to a door any distance from the parking lot, and leave black, black, black blobs and streaks that spread easily.

- **HOW HARD?** Depending on the dyes and other ingredients, can be very difficult to remove completely.

- **WHAT TO DO FIRST:** Gently pluck or scrape off as much of the tar off the surface as you can. Large, stubborn globs (as in carpeting) can be frozen and shattered, like chewing gum. (See pp. 72, 74, 209-210.)

- **WHAT TO DO NEXT**
  Fresh: Sponge repeatedly with dry spotter until the black stain is completely removed. Work from the outside toward the center, being careful not to spread the stain. If the stain is gone, apply laundry pre-treat and launder washables in hot water if safe for the fabric. For carpeting and upholstery, use a light, upward brushing motion, to pull the stain up and off the fibers; try not to rub it in deeper.
  Old/Dry: Apply petroleum jelly or De-Solv-it, and let it sit for 30 minutes to soften the stain, then treat as above.

• **IF THAT DOESN'T DO IT:** For washables, apply laundry pre-treat and keep wet for 20 minutes, then rinse with warm water. For dry cleanables, apply glycerin. Tamp if the fabric will tolerate it, then rinse. Don't launder washables until the stain is gone. If you can't get it all out, take the object in for professional spotting.

CAUTION: Don't use water until you've removed as much as possible with the dry solvents and oily spotters—water tends to set tar and make it spread even worse.

• **PREVENTION:** Whale the tar out of whoever did it!

tea (see Coffee)

STAIN:
Tobacco Smoke

• **WHAT IS IT?** Tiny particles of nicotine, tars, and resins suspended in carbon dioxide, carbon monoxide, and other gases.

• **WHAT CAN IT DO?** Make life short for the puffer and miserable for the cleaner. The sticky particles settle on surfaces and build up into an ugly yellow-brown layer with a strong odor.

• **HOW HARD?** That filthy film of smoke is easy enough to remove from fabrics you can wash and surfaces you can scrub. But lingering odor can be a challenge, especially in car interiors, upholstered furniture, and carpeting, where you can't reach all the particles trapped in padding materials, etc.

• **WHAT TO DO FIRST:** Put up "No Smoking" signs, so once you get the problem licked you won't have to do it again.

• **WHAT TO DO NEXT**
Washables: Mist with laundry pre-treat and wash in warm water. If odor remains, soak in mild vinegar solution and relaunder.

Dry Cleanables: Take in for professional dry cleaning— you'll never get all the smoke odor out without cleaning the whole thing.

Hard Surfaces: For walls and other water-safe surfaces, use a heavy-duty cleaner/degreaser in warm water. Add a little water-soluble deodorizer (available at janitorial-supply stores) to kill the odor. For windows with heavy smoke film, use half water and half alcohol.

Upholstery: For upholstered furniture and car interiors, shampoo with rug-and-upholstery shampoo (if safe for the fabric), to which you've added a little water-soluble deodorizer. If the furniture isn't safe for wet-cleaning, sponge the entire piece with dry spotter, or have it professionally dry cleaned. NOTE: Odor will still linger in the padding and inaccessible areas of the fabric. Airing out will help, but the only real cure is professional deodorizing (fogging with a smoke odor counteractant). Have carpeting professionally steam-cleaned, and ask the technician to add deodorizer to the cleaning solution.

• **PREVENTION:** See "What to Do First" above.

STAIN:

Tomato (fresh or canned tomatoes, tomato juice/sauce/ paste, tomato soup)

• **WHAT IS IT?** One of our most popular flavors, and most common stains. At least it's easy to see! What we're dealing with here is tomatoes, maybe salt, citric acid, and spices.

• **WHAT CAN IT DO?** Leave a reddish-brown blotch that will set with heat.

• **HOW HARD?** A bit balky when fresh; can be permanent if heat-set.

• **WHAT TO DO FIRST:** Gently scrape and blot to remove all you can, being careful not to force the stain deeper into the fabric.

• **WHAT TO DO NEXT**

Washables: Sponge with cool water, then with a solution of half vinegar and half water. Rinse with cool water. Apply a laundry pre-treat and wash in warm water. Air dry. If stain remains, soak in digestant for 30 minutes to an hour and relaunder.

Dry Cleanables: Sponge with cool water, then with a solution of half vinegar and half water. Rinse with cool water. If stain remains, apply a digestant paste (no digestant on silk or wool), let it sit without drying out for up to 30 minutes, then rinse with water.

• **IF THAT DOESN'T DO IT:** Bleach with hydrogen peroxide.

• **CAUTION:** Don't use hot water, hot-air drying, or iron until the stain is gone—heat will set it.

• **PREVENTION:** Remember that no matter how slow it flows on TV, in real life it slops, splatters, and spreads like crazy. And don't ever imagine you can eat a vine-ripened tomato tidily: Beefsteaks squirt and wedges drip and cherry tomatoes explode!

STAIN:
Toner (dry toner used in Xerox and other photocopy machines)

- **WHAT IS IT?** Particles of carbon black or ink, often encased in tiny plastic spheres.

- **WHAT CAN IT DO?** Fly around everywhere, making smudges on clothing, carpeting, and furniture. Can result in very difficult stains if the ink escapes the plastic encapsulation.

- **HOW HARD?** If the plastic coating remains intact, it's just a very fine black soil that needs to be removed extra-cautiously. If the ink is released by a solvent, pressure, or heat, you've got a dye stain on your hands.

- **WHAT TO DO FIRST:** Gently vacuum up all of the toner possible, being careful not to rub it deeper into the fabric. The more you get out before applying any liquid, the better!

- **WHAT TO DO NEXT**

Washables: Apply laundry pre-treat, launder in cold water, and air dry. Check to make sure all the toner has been removed before drying with heat or ironing. If stain remains, treat as for India ink.

Dry Cleanables: If the fabric will tolerate water, sponge the stain with neutral detergent solution before using any solvent. Dry cleaning solvents can dissolve the protective plastic coating in some toners and turn the ink loose. Rinse with cool water, feather the wet edge, and air dry. If stain remains, take in for professional dry cleaning.

• **CAUTION:** Don't use heat (hot water, hot dryer, or hot iron) until all traces of the toner are gone.

• **PREVENTION:** *Follow the directions* for adding toner; watch the repairman closely when he does it (he won't get toner on anything); or play dumb and let somebody else worry about that little "add toner" indicator.

---

typewriter ribbon (see Carbon Paper)
unknown stains (see Mystery Stains)
urine, animal or human (see Pet Stains)
varnish (see Paint—Oil-Base)

STAIN:
Vegetables

• **WHAT IS IT?** What mother told you to eat, not spill or spread around. (Contains vegetable dye, maybe oil, maybe tannin.)

• **WHAT CAN IT DO?** Attract rabbits, and leave a green or yellow stain.

• **HOW HARD?** Easy when fresh; harder as it ages.

• **WHAT TO DO FIRST:** Blot or scrape or remove all you can.

• **WHAT TO DO NEXT**
Fresh: Sponge with water. Apply laundry pre-treat to washables and launder in warm water. Sponge dry cleanables with wet spotter and a few drops of vinegar, then rinse with water and feather. Air dry. If stain remains, sponge with dry spotter.
Old/Dry: Sponge with dry spotter. If stain remains, treat as for fresh stain.

• **IF THAT DOESN'T DO IT:** Soak washables in digestant for 30 minutes to an hour, then launder in warm water. For dry cleanables, apply digestant paste, let it sit 30 minutes without drying out, then rinse with warm water. If stain remains, sponge with **alcohol** (test first). Some vegetable stains may require bleaching.

• **CAUTION:** Don't dry with heat or iron until the stain is gone—heat may set it.

• **PREVENTION:** Always keep your eye on them after you serve kale or anything similar. Move that high chair away from the wall and don your poncho when you break out the strained squash.

STAIN:
Vomit

- **WHAT IS IT?** Acids, digestive enzymes, partially digested food (and often an indication that we overdid it).

- **WHAT CAN IT DO?** Stomach juices exist to digest, and when they get on carpeting or clothes, they can "eat" and damage fabrics, too! Vomit can also out-odor any deodorizing spray in existence.

- **HOW HARD?** Upchuck is always unpleasant and untimely and on things not designed to be cleaned up quickly or easily. But you can get it out if you get right to it. Left to set, vomit can cause permanent color change.

- **WHAT TO DO FIRST:** Quickly scrape and blot up all you can, then flush the spot with water to dilute the acids and keep them from damaging the fabric. In carpeting or upholstery, sponge on water liberally and blot it back out.

• **WHAT TO DO NEXT**

Washables: Soak the item in a solution of one quart warm water to one teaspoon neutral detergent and two tablespoons of ammonia. Tamp or scrape to loosen the stain if the fabric will tolerate it. Rinse with cool water. If stain remains, soak in digestant 30 minutes to an hour, then launder in warm water. For colored stains, use a bleach safe for the fabric. .

Dry Cleanables: For fabrics that will tolerate water, apply wet spotter and a few drops of ammonia (no ammonia on silk or wool). Tamp or scrape if fabric will tolerate it. Sponge-rinse with cool water. If stain remains, apply digestant paste and leave it on there for 30 minutes, but don't let it dry out (no digestant on silk or wool). Rinse with warm water and feather. If stain remains, sponge with dry spotter; as a last resort, bleach with hydrogen peroxide.

Carpeting or Upholstery: Apply bacteria/enzyme digester, as for urine stains (see p. 261-262). If colored stain remains, treat as for Dye.

• **IF THAT DOESN'T DO IT:** It's probably a dye change caused by the acid—sorry!

• **CAUTION:** Vomit must be spotted with water. If you have a vomit stain on a dry-cleanable fabric with low water tolerance, such as silk or taffeta, take it in for professional spotting.

• **PREVENTION:** Put the one who's always carsick in the front seat, and pass up the strongly colored pet foods—the red dyes in them make for worse than usual vomit stains. Fido and Feline don't care what color their food is, anyway—they're color-blind.

STAIN:
Water Rings or White Marks on Furniture

- **WHAT IT IS?** A white ring or stain left on wood furniture by a wet glass or spilled liquid, or by heat. The heat or moisture chemically changes the finish and clouds it.

- **WHAT CAN IT DO?** Make your favorite furnishings look Tacky the Fourteenth or even make you decide to start crocheting doilies.

- **HOW HARD?** It can be easy as fading away by itself or as frustrating as a full-scale refinishing job.

- **WHAT TO DO FIRST:** Wait a day or two before you do anything. The mark may lighten as absorbed moisture evaporates.

- **WHAT TO DO NEXT:** Blemishes of this sort can usually be rubbed out using a mild abrasive mixed with a lubricant. Try one of these gentle combinations first: Johnson's Paste Wax and #00 steel wool; vegetable oil or mayonnaise with cigar ashes; white toothpaste with water. The idea is to make a paste and gently rub the finish with the abrasive (along the grain of the wood) until the spot blends in with the surrounding area. Have patience, and don't be too anxious to move up to a stronger abrasive—it may scratch. When finished, reapply the wax or furniture polish you normally use to the spot.

• **IF THAT DOESN'T DO IT:** Go to a more aggressive abrasive, such as rottenstone (available in paint stores) in linseed or salad oil. Or, as a last resort, use automotive polishing compound or automotive cleaner/polish. There is danger with these of scratching or even rubbing right through the finish, so take it easy, and quit immediately if it appears the finish is growing thin. You'll definitely have to apply wax or polish to hide the dull area these abrasives will leave.

• **PREVENTION:** On factory-finished furniture (which is usually lacquered), **use** that cute set of coasters you got in Cape Cod. Double-walled tumblers or the "high-rise" foam cocoons designed to keep canned drinks cold help control condensation, too. A coat of paste wax will help protect lacquered tabletops against damage. If you're finishing furniture yourself, use polyurethane or the new Scotchgard Wipe On Poly Finish, which resists alcohol, heat, and moisture better.

STAIN:
Water Spots on Fabric

• **WHAT IS IT?** The stain anyone can afford. Water spots usually form on fabrics that contain sizing or finishing agents.

The water displaces the sizing and is deposited around the edges of the spot in a ring or wavy line. Using water or wet spotters on dry-cleanable fabrics without feathering the edge will often result in a water spot. Fabrics most susceptible to water spotting are taffeta, moiré, and hard-finished silk or rayon.

• **WHAT CAN IT DO?** Leave your favorite silk blouse looking like a case of ringworm.

• **HOW HARD?** Comes out with regular laundering or dry cleaning, but can often be removed without doing the whole garment, using the procedures below.

• **WHAT TO DO FIRST:** Try rubbing the ring gently with the rounded back of a spoon, or lightly scratching with your fingernail or a stiff toothbrush. This will sometimes work the excess sizing out and lighten or completely remove the ring. Rubbing the fabric between the hands after scratching may help, too.

• **WHAT TO DO NEXT**
Washables: It's usually easiest to just launder or rewet the entire garment and dry as you normally would.
Dry Cleanables: Dampen the entire garment by waving it in the steam from a teakettle spout. If ironable, press while still damp, using a presscloth. If the ring remains, you'll have to have the garment professionally dry cleaned.

• **PREVENTION:** Quit trying to spot-clean silk and taffeta with water—it always leaves a water spot.

STAIN:
Water Stains on Ceilings

• **WHAT IS IT?** The result of water leaking down through a ceiling. The water carries dyes leached out of the roofing and insulation materials, and usually dries to a brown ring.

• **WHAT CAN IT DO?** Get you in the habit of casting your eyes downward.

• **HOW HARD?** Can range anywhere from disguising a drip to the whole ceiling caving in.

- **WHAT TO DO FIRST:** Try bleaching out the stain. This may remove it if it's not too bad. Spray on a 1:5 mixture of liquid chlorine bleach and water, or straight hydrogen peroxide.

- **WHAT TO DO NEXT**
Small spots that still show on white ceilings can be covered up by dabbing on a little white shoe polish.

- **IF THAT DOESN'T DO IT:** For large spots, seal the stain with pigmented shellac (available at paint stores) and paint to match the surrounding area after the shellac dries. If you don't prime with shellac first, the stain will bleed right through the paint. Spray-on touchup paint that needs no priming is also available to match most acoustic tile ceiling colors.

- **PREVENTION:** Fix the roof **before** monsoon season.

STAIN:
Wax (candle wax, paraffin, crayon, etc.)

- **WHAT IS IT?** Wax, possibly dye and perfume.

- **WHAT CAN IT DO?** The dyes in candles and crayons can cause permanent stains. And since it's dripped on while molten, the hot wax from a candle penetrates deep!

- **HOW HARD?** One of the tougher ones, and if the wax contains strong dye (such as red) it can be a real challenge.

- **WHAT TO DO FIRST:** For candle drips, first freeze the wax to harden it (see p. 72, 74). Then you can shatter the brittle mass by striking it briskly with the handle of a butter knife, and gently scrape to remove as much of the remaining residue as possible. Be careful not to distort or damage fibers.

- **WHAT TO DO NEXT**

Washables: After removing the bulk of the wax by freezing, place the stained area between two pieces of clean white cotton cloth or white paper towels. Iron with a warm iron to melt the wax and force it into the blotters. Change blotters and keep ironing until all the wax is gone. Apply laundry pre-treat and wash in hot water. Use bleach if safe for the fabric.

Dry Cleanables: After you've removed all you can by freezing, iron between blotters as above, then sponge the stain with dry spotter. Continue sponging until all traces of the wax are gone, and feather the edges.

Hard Surfaces: Crayon can be removed from painted walls, wood, wallpaper, floors, and most hard surfaces with WD-40; just spray and wipe.

- **IF THAT DOESN'T DO IT:** Spray with WD-40 and let it sit a few minutes. Tamp, then apply laundry pre-treat and launder washables in hot water if safe for the fabric. Remove WD-40 from dry cleanables with dry spotter.

- **PREVENTION:** Consider whether the candelabra has anything to help catch falling wax, not only how elegant it is. Put a table runner under candles if you really treasure your tabletop; get dripless candles and don't leave drafty windows open or fans running nearby, even so.

Take the time to find soap-base crayons and don't pass out crayons to amuse visiting kids!

---

white glue (see Glue—Water-Soluble)

STAIN:
Wine (red, rosé;
for white wine, see Liquor)

- **WHAT IS IT?** Alcohol, fruit, sugar, tannin.

- **What CAN IT DO?** Leave you with a red nose and permanent purple stains. The sugar in wine can also set with age and heat into a stubborn yellow spot.

- **HOW HARD?** Tough to very tough, depending on the wine and the fabric and how many mornings after it takes you to notice it. Aged stains can be impossible, especially if set by heat.

- **WHAT TO DO FIRST:** Blot to remove as much as possible, and immediately sponge with cool water until no more color is being removed. For sturdy fabrics, rub table salt into the stain, and treat with the boiling water method (see Fruit—Red). For fabrics that won't tolerate boiling water, follow the procedures below.

• **WHAT TO DO NEXT**

Washables: Sponge with wet spotter and a few drops of vinegar. Rinse with cool water. If stain remains, sponge with alcohol (test first). Apply laundry pre-treat and launder in cool water; air dry. If stain remains, soak in digestant for 30 minutes to an hour and rewash in warm water.

Dry Cleanables: Sponge with wet spotter and a few drops of vinegar as long as any wine color is being removed. Rinse with cool water. If stain remains, sponge with alcohol (dilute 1:1 with water for acetate; test for colorfastness on any fabric). Rinse with water. If stain remains, apply digestant paste (no digestant on silk or wool), let sit for 30 minutes without drying out, then rinse with water. Feather to avoid water spots.

• **IF THAT DOESN'T DO IT:** Bleach with as strong a bleach as the fabric will tolerate. Valuable pieces should be taken in for expert spotting and cleaning.

• **CAUTION:** Don't use hot water, dry with heat, or iron before you're sure it's gone—heat will set sugar stains. Don't use soap.

• **PREVENTION:** Put the cork in the trash or the ash tray—not on the tablecloth. Practice till you can pour like a wine steward—slowly, twisting the bottle neck to the side as you finish (so any drips end up inside).

---

wood glue (see Glue—Water-Soluble).

STAIN:
Wood Stain

• **WHAT IS IT?** Pigments and dyes in a solvent or water-emulsion base.

• **WHAT CAN IT DO?** Live up to its name. Talk about a stain—this was created to color things, and that's what it does—usually permanently.

• **HOW HARD?** The worst—if it's on something porous, you aren't likely to get it out.

• **WHAT TO DO FIRST:** Don't let it dry! If you can flush it out while it's still wet, there's a chance of complete removal. If you let it dry, it's probably a lost cause.

• **WHAT TO DO NEXT:** Treat oil-based stain like Oil-Based Paint, and water-based stain like Water-Based Paint. (See Paint—Oil-Based and Paint—Water-Based.)

• **IF THAT DOESN'T DO IT:** Treat as a Dye stain.

• **PREVENTION:** Make sure all furniture legs have glides or rubber or plastic coasters, and you won't have wood stain leaching out of furniture legs onto carpet. And if you have to put furniture back onto freshly cleaned carpet, place a square of plastic, foil, or unprinted cardboard under the legs until the carpet is good and dry.

Worcestershire sauce (see Soy Sauce)
yellowing of laundry (see Chapter 2)

Acknowledgments

Writing about stains takes as many "helps" as removing them. My sincere thanks to all the stain crew:

Gary Luke, executive editor of New American Library, for the original idea and for his selfless exploration of stain possibilities.

Mark Browning, my partner and cleaning consultant, who cut through the terrifying thicket of technical questions that surround stain removal.

Carol Cartaino, my agent and worst taskmaster (and owner of more stainables than Bloomingdale's).

Tobi Haynes, my production manager, who fed it all into the computer and saw that it all happened on time.

Craig LaGory, the illustrator, who stays awake nights creating splotch monsters and thinking of ways to make plain old type come alive.

Della Gibbs and **Linda Hegg,** researchers, who helped crack some of the more elusive stain-removal mysteries.

Maytag, for their excellent information on fabrics and their care.

Procter & Gamble, Unilever, Johnson Wax, R. R. Street & Co., many other manufacturers, and the **Soap & Detergent Association,** for help in understanding their specific stain-removal products and strategies.

The chemists at National Sanitary Supply in Los Angeles, who answered all my questions about why chemicals do the things they do.

The many helpful launderers, dry cleaners, carpet and upholstery technicians, and professional cleaning associates who spent time sharing the tricks of their trade with me.

And I wouldn't want to forget the fast food companies who made it all necessary, and the manufacturers of anything red.

Index

About the Author

Don Aslett, America's foremost authority on "clean," has been advising Americans since 1981 how to kick kitchen grease out forever, whittle the wax buildup off floors and furniture, and tame the rankest of restrooms. For thirty-three years he and the professional cleaning company he founded, Varsity Contractors, have cleaned in every situation and setting imaginable, commercial and domestic—bachelor pads and eight-child homes; boats, planes, and buses; hotels, schools, offices, and factories; log cabins and million-dollar mansions; even cleaned after fires, floods, and tornadoes.

He's shared the how-tos of it all with the world in a total of ten books to date. His first best-seller, *Is There Life After Housework?*, a primer of professional cleaning methods for the homemaker, has sold over half a million copies and been translated into five languages. He tackled the biggest hidden problem in cleaning, household junk, in *Clutter's Last Stand*. He took on the unimaginable topic of how to get men to do their share of the housework in *Who Says It's a Woman's Job to*

Clean? He took cleaning right to the mat in a book on designing and building cleaning out of a home: *Make Your House Do the Housework.* He solved the problem of how to live a clean life with pets in *Pet Clean-Up Made Easy.* He shared the expertise that put his cleaning company in the top 2 percent nationwide in *Cleaning Up for a Living.* And he answered a total of two hundred of the home cleaner's most perplexing questions in *Do I Dust or Vacuum First?* and *How Do I Clean the Moosehead?* And now he takes on the hottest topic in cleaning—stain removal!

Don likes to stay in close touch with American cleaners—and his readers. You can be on his Clean Report newsletter list—free—and receive catalogs of professional cleaning supplies, directions for betting cleaning, or further information on any cleaning topic, by writing to Don Aslett's Cleaning Center, PO Box 39, Pocatello, ID 83204. If you're interested in seminars, workshops, classes, or convention speaker call Don's office at 208-232-6212.